OPPOSING
VIEWPOINTS®
SERIES

Artificial Intelligence

Other Books of Related Interest:

At Issue Series
Wave and Tidal Power

Current Controversies Series
Forensic Technology
Human Genetics
Nuclear Energy

Global Viewpoints Series
The Internet

Introducing Issues with Opposing Viewpoints Series
Video Games

Opposing Viewpoints Series
The Armed Forces

"Congress shall make
no law . . . abridging
the freedom of speech,
or of the press."

First Amendment to the US Constitution

The basic foundation of our democracy is the First Amendment guarantee of freedom of expression. The Opposing Viewpoints Series is dedicated to the concept of this basic freedom and the idea that it is more important to practice it than to enshrine it.

Artificial Intelligence

Noah Berlatsky, Book Editor

GREENHAVEN PRESS
A part of Gale, Cengage Learning

Detroit • New York • San Francisco • New Haven, Conn • Waterville, Maine • London

GALE
CENGAGE Learning

Christine Nasso, *Publisher*
Elizabeth Des Chenes, *Managing Editor*

For more information, contact:
Greenhaven Press
27500 Drake Rd.
Farmington Hills, MI 48331-3535
Or you can visit our Internet site at gale.cengage.com

For product information and technology assistance, contact us at

Gale Customer Support, 1-800-877-4253
For permission to use material from this text or product, submit all requests online at
www.cengage.com/permissions

Further permissions questions can be emailed to permissionrequest@cengage.com

Articles in Greenhaven Press anthologies are often edited for length to meet page requirements. In addition, original titles of these works are changed to clearly present the main thesis and to explicitly indicate the author's opinion. Every effort is made to ensure that Greenhaven Press accurately reflects the original intent of the authors. Every effort has been made to trace the owners of copyrighted material.

Cover image copyright © by imredesiuk/Shutterstock.com.

LIBRARY OF CONGRESS CATALOGING-IN-PUBLICATION DATA
Artificial intelligence / Noah Berlatsky, book editor. p. cm. -- (Opposing viewpoints) Includes bibliographical references and index. ISBN 978-0-7377-5709-5 (hardcover) -- ISBN 978-0-7377-5710-1 (pbk.) 1. Artificial intelligence. I. Berlatsky, Noah. Q335.A78582 2011 006.3--dc22   2010051822

Printed in the United States of America
1 2 3 4 5 6 7 15 14 13 12 11

Contents

Chapter 3: What Ethical Issues Are Raised by Artificial Intelligence?

Chapter 4: What Are Some Valuable Applications of Artificial Intelligence?

Why Consider Opposing Viewpoints?

> "The only way in which a human being can make some approach to knowing the whole of a subject is by hearing what can be said about it by persons of every variety of opinion and studying all modes in which it can be looked at by every character of mind. No wise man ever acquired his wisdom in any mode but this."
>
> John Stuart Mill

In our media-intensive culture it is not difficult to find differing opinions. Thousands of newspapers and magazines and dozens of radio and television talk shows resound with differing points of view. The difficulty lies in deciding which opinion to agree with and which "experts" seem the most credible. The more inundated we become with differing opinions and claims, the more essential it is to hone critical reading and thinking skills to evaluate these ideas. Opposing Viewpoints books address this problem directly by presenting stimulating debates that can be used to enhance and teach these skills. The varied opinions contained in each book examine many different aspects of a single issue. While examining these conveniently edited opposing views, readers can develop critical thinking skills such as the ability to compare and contrast authors' credibility, facts, argumentation styles, use of persuasive techniques, and other stylistic tools. In short, the Opposing Viewpoints Series is an ideal way to attain the higher-level thinking and reading skills so essential in a culture of diverse and contradictory opinions.

In addition to providing a tool for critical thinking, Opposing Viewpoints books challenge readers to question their own strongly held opinions and assumptions. Most people form their opinions on the basis of upbringing, peer pressure, and personal, cultural, or professional bias. By reading carefully balanced opposing views, readers must directly confront new ideas as well as the opinions of those with whom they disagree. This is not to simplistically argue that everyone who reads opposing views will—or should—change his or her opinion. Instead, the series enhances readers' understanding of their own views by encouraging confrontation with opposing ideas. Careful examination of others' views can lead to the readers' understanding of the logical inconsistencies in their own opinions, perspective on why they hold an opinion, and the consideration of the possibility that their opinion requires further evaluation.

Evaluating Other Opinions

To ensure that this type of examination occurs, Opposing Viewpoints books present all types of opinions. Prominent spokespeople on different sides of each issue as well as well-known professionals from many disciplines challenge the reader. An additional goal of the series is to provide a forum for other, less known, or even unpopular viewpoints. The opinion of an ordinary person who has had to make the decision to cut off life support from a terminally ill relative, for example, may be just as valuable and provide just as much insight as a medical ethicist's professional opinion. The editors have two additional purposes in including these less known views. One, the editors encourage readers to respect others' opinions—even when not enhanced by professional credibility. It is only by reading or listening to and objectively evaluating others' ideas that one can determine whether they are worthy of consideration. Two, the inclusion of such viewpoints encourages the important critical thinking skill of objectively evaluating an author's credentials and bias. This evaluation will illuminate an author's reasons for taking a particular stance on an issue and will aid in readers' evaluation of the author's ideas.

It is our hope that these books will give readers a deeper understanding of the issues debated and an appreciation of the complexity of even seemingly simple issues when good and honest people disagree. This awareness is particularly important in a democratic society such as ours in which people enter into public debate to determine the common good. Those with whom one disagrees should not be regarded as enemies but rather as people whose views deserve careful examination and may shed light on one's own.

Thomas Jefferson once said that "difference of opinion leads to inquiry, and inquiry to truth." Jefferson, a broadly educated man, argued that "if a nation expects to be ignorant and free ... it expects what never was and never will be." As individuals and as a nation, it is imperative that we consider the opinions of others and examine them with skill and discernment. The Opposing Viewpoints Series is intended to help readers achieve this goal.

David L. Bender and Bruno Leone,
Founders

Introduction

"Most of us came to technology through science fiction; our imaginations remain secretly moved by science-fictional ideas."

—Jason Pontin,
"On Science Fiction,"
Technology Review, March 2007

People have been fascinated with the idea of artificial intelligence (AI) for hundreds of years. In fact, the first science fiction novel, Mary Shelley's *Frankenstein* (1818), focused on a scientist who builds an artificial, intelligent creature. According to a July 23, 2007, article on the *Invasion Plans* website (http://dev.marzopolis.com/), "Although not possessing many of the characteristics of modern robots and A.I., the story immediately set the tone for the way artificial life was depicted in literary and pop culture." The article also notes, "As in *Frankenstein*, some of the earliest stories and films portrayed [creatures with artificial intelligence] as things to fear and destroy." In fact, Shelley's artificial monster is not exactly evil, though he does commit murder when he is rejected by his creator.

Today AI is most often associated not with Frankenstein, but with robots. The name "robot" was first popularized by Czech playwright Karel Čapek (1890–1938). In 1921, Čapek's play *R.U.R.* featured artificial creatures who worked as slaves. Čapek called these artificial laborers "robots," after *robota*, which was the name for serfs in Eastern Europe. "The robots in *R.U.R.* are created by a scientist, inevitably a mad one, to free the humans from the drudgery and elevate them to the higher spheres of learning. When things go wrong and there is an uprising, it resembles all those others staged by slaves in various places throughout the centuries, however, with an even more profound impact," according to Voyen Koreis in an article on www.capekbrothers.net.

Not all fictional robots have been a threat to humanity. One of the most famous and influential writers of robot stories, Isaac Asimov (1920–1992), specifically set out to get away from the Frankenstein/Čapek model of robots attacking humans. "This frequent cliche of early science fiction held that robots were vengeful monsters fated to rise up against their former masters in murderous wrath. [Asimov's] short stories recast robots as tools—incredibly complex tools, to be sure, but nonetheless tools that . . . allowed for a more cerebral, layered exploration of the differences between humans and robots," according to Alasdair Wilkins writing in a May 24, 2009, article on the website io9.com. Asimov is most famous not for a particular story or novel, but rather for his invention of what he called the "Three Laws of Robotics." These laws governed the behavior of robots in his world. The laws stated:

1. "A robot may not injure a human being or, through inaction, allow a human being to come to harm.

2. A robot must obey orders given to it by human beings, except where such orders would conflict with the First Law.

3. A robot must protect its own existence as long as such protection does not conflict with the First or Second Law."

Just as *Frankenstein*'s monster is not realistic, so Asimov's laws are not used by actual roboticists. However, they made for many interesting stories. For instance, in the 1985 novel *Robots and Empire*, a robot must decide whether protecting humanity should override the First Law's injunction that no individual humans should be harmed.

Since Asimov, one of the most well known science fiction AI creations has been the Terminator. The Terminator first appeared in the 1984 film *Terminator*, directed by James Cameron. A second film, *Terminator 2: Judgment Day*, appeared in 1991 and also was influential. The Terminator also inspired another film and a television series.

The Terminator films imagined a future in which an artificially intelligent defense network, the so-called Skynet, "decides—in a moment of binary brilliance—that the quickest path to peace is genocide," according to Erik Sofge in an October 1, 2009, article in *Popular Mechanics*. Even after Skynet launches a nuclear apocalypse, however, a group of human rebels fight on. To undermine these rebels, Skynet sends killer robots, or Terminators, back into the past. The rebels also send robots back into the past, and the series features good robots fighting bad robots for the future of humanity. The series has been popular enough that references to "Terminator" or "Skynet" are a frequent shorthand means of referring to robot apocalypse.

There have been many other important fictional uses of AI over the years. The 1968 film *2001: A Space Odyssey*, featured a famously homicidal computer intelligence called HAL. The *Star Wars* franchise, the first film of which appeared in 1977, featured two friendly iconic robots, R2D2 and C3PO. Television shows such as *Star Trek* and *Battlestar Galactica* also have included AI characters, both as heroes and villains.

AI researchers have not created a real Frankenstein, but they do struggle with many practical and ethical issues that would have been familiar to writers such as Mary Shelley (1797–1851) or Isaac Asimov. In *Opposing Viewpoints: Artificial Intelligence*, authors confront these issues in four chapters: Is It Possible to Develop Artificial Intelligence? What Does the Turing Test Reveal About Artificial Intelligence? What Ethical Issues Are Raised by Artificial Intelligence? and What Are Some Valuable Applications of Artificial Intelligence? The following viewpoints examine both the imagined future and more realistic possibilities for artificial intelligence.

 CHAPTER 1

Is It Possible to Develop Artificial Intelligence?

Chapter Preface

Philosophers and scientists disagree about whether it is possible to develop artificial intelligence (AI). In part, this is because they disagree about what qualifies as artificial intelligence. In order to better define "artificial intelligence," philosophers have split AI into two concepts: weak AI and strong AI.

"[T]he assertion that machines could act *as if* they were intelligent is called the weak AI hypothesis by philosophers, and the assertion that machines that do so are *actually* thinking (not just *simulating* thinking) is called the strong AI hypothesis," according to Stuart Russell and Peter Norvig in their 2010 book *Artificial Intelligence: A Modern Approach*, 3rd ed. Russell and Norvig go on to note that "Most AI researchers take the weak AI hypothesis for granted, and don't care about the strong AI hypothesis—as long as their program works, they don't care whether you call it a simulation of intelligence or real intelligence."

As the definition above suggests, programmers already have achieved many different kinds of weak AI. Search-engine software such as Google, for example, could be considered an example of weak AI. "A classic example of an AI application that many would consider intelligent in some form is computer chess," according to H. Peter Alesso and Craig F. Smith in their 2006 book *Thinking on the Web: Berners-Lee, Gödel, and Turing*. Alesso and Smith also point to drive-by-wire cars and speech recognition software as examples of weak AI. Such successes demonstrate, they say, that "some thinking-life features can be added to computers to make them more useful tools."

In the 1950s, many scientists believed humans could achieve not just weak AI, but strong AI. However, the creation of machines that think like humans has proved far more difficult than it seemed at first. "Some argue that we have not yet built a machine that possesses the intellectual capability of an ant, and that the prospect of an AI worthy of the designation of 'human' remains an elusive dream," according to Jay Friedenberg and Gordon Silverman in their 2005 book *Cognitive Science: An Introduction to the Study of Mind.* However, Friedenberg and Silverman note that many researchers continue to hope for the development of strong AI.

In the viewpoints that follow, authors present different perspectives on how success in AI should be defined and whether such success is possible.

"It seems plausible that with technology we can, in the fairly near future, create (or become) creatures who surpass humans in every intellectual and creative dimension."

The Development of Artificial Intelligence Is Imminent

Peter Moon and Vernor Vinge

Vernor Vinge is a science fiction author and a retired San Diego State University professor of mathematics; Peter Moon, who interviews Vinge, is a writer for the online publication Computerworld. *In the following viewpoint, Vinge argues that sometime, not too long after 2020, artificial intelligence will surpass human intelligence, allowing for unimaginable advances. Vinge says there are dangers in this scenario, because robots may be immoral. However, he concludes that overall advances in technology are much more likely to benefit humans than to destroy them.*

As you read, consider the following questions:

1. What comparison does Vinge use to describe how unimaginable events beyond the singularity would be?

Peter Moon and Vernor Vinge, "AI Will Surpass Human Intelligence After 2020," *Computerworld*, May 7, 2007. Reprinted with permission.

2. When is Vinge's novel *Rainbow's End* set, and what does he imagine the world to be like at that time?

3. Does Vinge think advances in technology will result in more tyranny or more freedom, and what is his rationale?

Vernor Vinge, 62, is a pioneer in artificial intelligence, who in a recent interview warned about the risks and opportunities that an electronic super-intelligence would offer to mankind.

Vinge is a retired San Diego State University professor of mathematics, computer scientist, and science fiction author. He is well-known for his 1993 manifesto, "The Coming Technological Singularity," in which he argues that exponential growth in technology means a point will be reached where the consequences are unknown. Vinge still believes in this future, which he thinks would come anytime after 2020.

Exactly 10 years ago, in May 1997, Deep Blue won the chess tournament against Gary Kasparov. Was that the first glimpse of a new kind of intelligence?

I think there was clever programming in Deep Blue, but the predictable success came mainly from the ongoing trends in computer hardware improvement. The result was a better-than-human performance in a single, limited problem area. In the future, I think that improvements in both software and hardware will bring success in other intellectual domains.

In 1993 you gave your famous, almost prophetic, speech on "Technological Singularity." Can you please describe the concept of Singularity?

It seems plausible that with technology we can, in the fairly near future, create (or become) creatures who surpass humans in every intellectual and creative dimension. Events beyond such an event—such a singularity—are as unimaginable to us as opera is to a flatworm.

Do you still believe in the coming singularity?

I think it's the most likely non-catastrophic outcome of the next few decades.

Does the explosion of the Internet and grid computing ultimately accelerate this event?

Yes. There are other possible paths to the Singularity, but at the least, computer + communications + people provide a healthy setting for further intellectual leaps.

When intelligent machines finally appear, what will they look like?

Most likely they will be less visible than computers are now. They would mostly operate via the networks and the processors built into the ordinary machines of our everyday life. On the other hand, the results of their behaviour could be very spectacular changes in our physical world. (One exception: mobile robots, even before the Singularity, will probably become very impressive—with devices that are more agile and coordinated than human athletes, even in open-field situations.)

How would we be certain about its conscience?

The hope and the peril is that these creatures would be our "mind children." As with any child, there is a question of how moral they may grow up to be, and yet there is good reason for hope. (Of course, the peril is that these particular children are much more powerful than natural ones.)

Stephen Hawking defended in 2001 the genetic enhancing of our species in order to compete with intelligent machines. Do you believe it would be feasible, even practical?

I think it's both practical and positive—and subject to the same qualitative concerns as the computer risks. In the long run I don't think organic biology can keep up with hardware. On the other hand, organic biology is robust in different ways than machine hardware. The survival of Life is best served by preserving and enhancing both strategies.

Science Fiction and the Singularity

Reason [magazine]: *What is the role of science fiction in helping us cope with a transformation you believe many of us will live to see?*

Vernor Vinge: I think science fiction can have all the power of conventional literature, but with the added potential for providing us with vivid, emotionally grounded insights into the future and into alternative scenarios. Speaking grandiosely, science fiction might be taken as having the role for humanity that sleep dreaming has for the individual. Sleep dreams are mostly nonsense, but sometimes we wake up with the stark realization that we have underestimated a possibility or a goodness or a threat.

Mike Godwin and Vernor Vinge,
"Superhuman Imagination,"
Reason, *May 2007. http://reason.com.*

Could nanotechnology, genetic engineering and quantum computers represent a threat to Mankind, as Bill Joy, the former Sun executive, warned in 2000 with his "Why the future doesn't need us"?

The world (and the universe) is full of mortal threats. Technology is the source of some of those threats—but it has also protected us from others. I believe that technology itself is life's surest response to the ongoing risks.

Right now the Pentagon is employing 5,000 robots in Iraq, patrolling cities, disarming explosives or making reconnaissance flights. The next step is allowing them to carry weapons. Does this lead to a "Terminator" scenario?

That's conceivable, though not a reason for turning away from robotics in general. Old-fashioned thermonuclear world war and some types of biowarfare are much simpler, more likely, and probably more deadly than the "Terminator" scenario.

You set the plot of your last novel, Rainbows End, *in 2025. It's a world where people Google all the time, everywhere, using wearable computers, and omnipresent sensors. Do you think this is a plausible future?*

It was about the most plausible (non-catastrophic) 2025 scenario that I could think of.

It is a little scary, isn't it? Is this the great conspiracy against human freedom?

Before the personal computer, most people thought computers were the great enemy of freedom. When the PC came along, many people realized that millions of computers in the hands of citizens were a defence against tyranny. Now in the new millennium, we see how governments can use networks for overarching surveillance and enforcement; that is scary.

But one of the ideas I am trying to get at with *Rainbows End* is the possibility that government abuse may turn out to be irrelevant: As technology becomes more important, there governments need to provide the illusion of freedom for the millions of people who must be happy and creative in order for the economy to succeed. Altogether, these people are more diverse and resourceful (and even more coordinated!) than any government. Online databases, computer networks, and social networks give this trend an enormous boost. In the end, that "illusion of freedom" may have to be more like the real thing than has ever been true in history. With the Internet, the people may achieve a new kind of populism, powered by deep knowledge, self-interest so broad as to reasonably be called tolerance, and an automatic, preternatural vigilance.

| "Neuroscientists can't mimic brains be-
cause they lack basic understanding of
how brains work; they don't know what
to include in a simulation and what to
leave out."

Artificial Brains Are Imminent . . . Not!

John Horgan

John Horgan is director of the Center for Science Writings at the Stevens Institute of Technology. In the following viewpoint, he argues that current brain simulations do not come close to imitating actual brain functions. Horgan says scientists have little sense of how brains work. Therefore, claims that computers will soon mimic brain functions is, according to Horgan, wishful thinking.

As you read, consider the following questions:

1. Why does Terry Sejnowski say computers will soon be able to mimic the brain's workings?

2. According to Horgan, the brain simulation projects of researchers Markram and Modha have neural-signaling patterns that resemble those of real brains doing what?

3. How does Horgan say that brains and computers may encode information differently?

Scientists are on the verge of building an artificial brain! How do I know? Terry Sejnowski of the Salk Institute said so right here on *ScientificAmerican.com*. He wrote that the goal of reverse-engineering the brain—which the National Academy of Engineering recently posed as one of its "grand challenges"—is "becoming increasingly plausible." Scientists are learning more and more about the brain, and computers are becoming more and more powerful. So naturally computers will soon be able to mimic the brain's workings. So says Sejnowski.

Sejnowski is a very smart guy, whom I've interviewed several times over the years about the mysteries of the brain. But I respectfully—hell, disrespectfully, Terry can take it—disagree with his prediction that artificial brains are imminent. Sejnowski's own article shows how implausible his prediction is. He describes two projects—both software programs running on powerful supercomputers—that represent the state of the art in brain simulation. On the one hand, you have the "cat brain" constructed by IBM researcher Dharmendra Modha; his simulation contains about as many neurons as a cat's brain does organized into roughly the same architecture. On the other hand, you have the Blue Brain Project of Henry Markram, a neuroscientist at the Ecole Polytechnique Fédérale de Lausanne.

Markram's simulation contains neurons and synaptic connections that are much more detailed than those in Modha's program. Markram recently bashed Modha for "mass deception," arguing that Modha's neurons and synapses are so simple that they don't deserve to be called simulations.

Modha's program is "light years away from a cat brain, not even close to an ant's brain in complexity," Markram complained.

Talk about the pot calling the kettle black. Last year Markram stated, "It is not impossible to build a human brain and we can do it in 10 years." If Modha's simulation is "light years" away from reality, so is Markram's. Neither program includes "sensory inputs or motor outputs," Sejnowski points out, and their neural-signaling patterns resemble those of brains sleeping or undergoing an epileptic seizure. In other words, neither Modha nor Markram can mimic even the simplest operations of a healthy, awake, embodied brain.

The simulations of Modha and Markram are about as brain-like as one of those plastic brains that neuroscientists like to keep on their desks. The plastic brain has all the parts that a real brain does, it's roughly the same color and it has about as many molecules in it. OK, say optimists, the plastic brain doesn't actually perceive, emote, plan or decide, but don't be so critical! Give the researchers time! Another analogy: Current brain simulations resemble the "planes" and "radios" that Melanesian cargo-cult tribes built out of palm fronds, coral and coconut shells after being occupied by Japanese and American troops during World War II. "Brains" that can't think are like "planes" that can't fly.

In spite of all our sophisticated instruments and theories, our own brains are still as magical and mysterious to us as a cargo plane was to those Melanesians. Neuroscientists can't mimic brains because they lack basic understanding of how brains work; they don't know what to include in a simulation and what to leave out. Most simulations assume that the basic physical unit of the brain is the neuron, and the basic unit of information is the electrochemical action potential, or spike, emitted by the neuron. A typical brain contains 100 billion cells, and each cell is linked via dendrites and synapses to as many as 100,000 others. Assuming that each synapse processes

The Singularity Is a Fantasy

Perhaps the old joke is right after all: If the brain were simple enough for us to understand, we wouldn't be smart enough to understand it.

Let's face it. The singularity [that is, the idea that artificial intelligence will surpass human intelligence, leading to unimaginable advances] is a religious rather than a scientific vision. The science-fiction writer Ken MacLeod has dubbed it "the rapture for nerds," an allusion to the end-time, when Jesus whisks the faithful to heaven and leaves us sinners behind.

Such yearning for transcendence, whether spiritual or technological, is all too understandable. Both as individuals and as a species, we face deadly serious problems, including terrorism, nuclear proliferation, overpopulation, poverty, famine, environmental degradation, climate change, resource depletion, and AIDS. Engineers and scientists should be helping us face the world's problems and find solutions to them, rather than indulging in escapist, pseudoscientific fantasies like the singularity.

John Horgan, "The Consciousness Conundrum,"
IEEE Spectrum, June 2008. http://spectrum.ieee.org.

one action potential per second and that these transactions represent the brain's computational output, then the brain performs at least one quadrillion operations per second.

Computers are fast approaching this information-processing capacity, leading to claims by artificial intelligence enthusiast Ray Kurzweil and others that computers will soon not just equal but surpass our brains in cognitive power. But the brain may be processing information at many levels below and above that of individual neurons and synapses. Moreover, scientists have no idea how the brain encodes information. Unlike computers, which employ a single, static machine code that translates electrical pulses into information, brains may employ many different "neural codes," which may be constantly changing in response to new experiences.

Go back a decade or two—or five or six—and you will find artificial intelligence pioneers like Marvin Minsky and Herbert Simon proclaiming, because of exciting advances in brain and computer science: Artificial brains are coming! They're going to save us! Or destroy us! Someday, these prophecies may come true, but there is no reason to believe them now.

> "There is no inherent theological conflict between a biblical view of personhood and work in artificial intelligence, nor would successes in this field undermine human value or the doctrine of the image of God."

Christianity Allows for the Possibility of Artificial Intelligence

Russell C. Bjork

Russell C. Bjork is professor of computer science at Gordon College in Wenham, Massachusetts. In the following viewpoint, he argues that theologically the soul may emerge from bodily processes. He also argues that, in Christian teaching, human specialness need not be based on what humans are, but rather on what God intends for them. As a result, Bjork says, an artificial intelligence could have a soul and would not diminish the theological basis of human worth. Bjork adds that Christianity's insights into intelligence may help to suggest how to achieve artificial intelligence and what its limits might be.

Russell C. Bjork, "Artificial Intelligence and the Soul," *Perspectives on Science and Christian Faith*, vol. 60, no. 2, June 2008, pp. 95–101. Reprinted with permission.

As you read, consider the following questions:

1. From what does Bjork say personhood may emerge?

2. Bjork says that human worth is not based on our constitution, but rather on what?

3. Why does Bjork say that Hans Moravec and Ray Kurzweil may be guilty of idolatry?

For many years, thinkers have speculated about creating an artifact that deserves to be called a person. Moreover, intelligent robots or androids of various sorts have been prominent in works of popular culture (e.g., Commander Data of *Star Trek: The Next Generation*, R2D2 or C3PO of *Star Wars*, Andrew Martin of the Isaac Asimov short story which was later turned into the film *The Bicentennial Man*, or David of *Artificial Intelligence*). Is creation of such an artifact theoretically possible? Certainly there are many today who believe this to be the case. For example, Rodney Brooks, the director of the Computer Science and Artificial Intelligence Laboratory at MIT [Massachusetts Institute of Technology], claims that "the question then is when, not if, we will build self-reproducing intelligent robots." However, some Christians have seen this possibility as contradicting Christian doctrines concerning humanity, such as the nature of the soul or humans being made in the image of God. As one writer put it, "I fully grant that my theology would crumble with the advent of intelligent machines."

Theological Questions About Artificial Intelligence

Is there an inherent conflict between biblical teaching and the idea of an intelligent artifact? Or is it rather the case that Christian theology has something to say about how one might approach such a goal? Note that these are phrased as theological questions, not technological ones. No existing systems even come close to the kind of intelligence displayed by, say, Commander Data, and there is no hard evidence that such a system will exist in the near future, if ever. But one who believes in this possibility can legitimately point to a long history of technologies that we take for granted today, that were once believed to be impossible. The question I wish to address here is whether Christian theology has any necessary stake in the impossibility of creating an artifact that deserves to be called a person, on the one hand, or has anything to say about how one might pursue such an objective, on the other hand. In particular, I want to address three issues:

1. Is there a conflict between artificial intelligence and biblical teaching about the origin of the human soul?

2. Is there a conflict between artificial intelligence and biblical teaching about human worth or our being created in the image of God?

3. Does biblical teaching about human personhood have any implications for work in artificial intelligence?

Artificial Intelligence and the Origin of the Soul

That Christian doctrine and artificial intelligence might conflict has been part of the discussion from the outset. The earliest paper to espouse what we now call "artificial intelligence" (though it did not actually use this phrase) was Alan Turing's "Computing Machinery and Intelligence." Turing devoted much of the paper to addressing various objections to the idea of "thinking machines," of which the first is what he called "The Theological Objection":

> Thinking is a function of man's immortal soul. God has given an immortal soul to every man and woman, but not to any other animal or to machines. Hence no animal or machine can think.

This view was not Turing's (He explicitly stated, "I am unable to accept any part of this."); rather, he was attempting to state and respond to an objection to his thesis that he assumed others would have.

This objection does not really concern the *nature* of the soul, but rather the *origin* of the soul. It considers God's creative acts to be of two kinds—material and immaterial. Technology has access only to what belongs in the realm of the former, but human personhood involves an immaterial component that only God could create. If this overall understanding is correct, then there would appear to be a conflict between biblical teaching and technological efforts to create an artifact that can rightly be called a person. Is this, however, an accurate understanding of biblical teaching?

The creation of humanity is described in Gen. [Genesis] 2:7 (KJV [King James Version of the Bible]): "And the LORD God formed man of the dust of the ground, and breathed into his nostrils the breath of life (*neshamah hayim*); and man became a living soul (*nephesh hayah*)." Many Christians understand this to speak of what are, in effect, two separate creative acts by God first, God formed man's body; and then—separately—God created man's soul (understood as an immaterial component part of humans, "an immortal though created essence, which is [man's] nobler part"). On this view, the former is seen as physical—perhaps an immediate act of God or perhaps a process mediated through a mechanism such as evolution by natural selection—but the latter is seen as involving a divine act that lies outside the material realm.

However, this does not seem to be what the text actually, says. It does not say that God made man's *body* of dust. It says he made *man* of dust. Neither is the "breath of life" something immaterial which sets humanity apart from animals. When the phrase *neshamah hayim* next occurs (in Gen. 7:22), it explicitly refers to all creatures (both humans and beast) drowned by the flood, describing them as those who had "the breath of life." Moreover, the text does not say that man "received" a living soul, but rather "became" a living soul—which seems better understood as meaning a living organism that has animate life rather than as an immaterial substance which sets humans apart from other creatures. (It does not make sense to say that man "*became* an immaterial substance"; moreover it is not clear that *nephesh* ever has the latter meaning.) In the first two chapters of Genesis, *nephesh hayah* is used a total of six times; in the remaining occurrences (1:20, 21, 24, 30; 2:19), it explicitly refers to nonhuman creatures. (Indeed, many newer translations translate *nephesh hayah* in Gen. 2:7 with a phrase like "living being" for this reason.) In order to read this text as teaching two kinds of divine creative acts, one must implicitly substitute words that are not there for those that appear—e.g., "man's body" instead of "man," "immaterial soul" instead of "breath of (physical) life," "received" in place of "became," and "immaterial soul" in place of "living (animate) being." We will return later to the crucial point of the text: what makes humans special is not what humanity *is*, but rather it is God's *relationship* to us based on his purpose for making us.

An attractive alternative is to understand the immaterial aspect of humans (personhood) as an emergent phenomenon: personhood emerges from the interaction of the neurons in the brain. While this is certainly not the historical understanding (nor could it be, given that knowledge of the workings of the brain is fairly recent), it is not at all inconsistent with the silence of Scripture as to the details of exactly *how* God created a race of beings in his image. A Christian who holds an emergent view of personhood affirms the reality of God's creatorship of persons—in much the same way that he or she affirms the reality of God's ultimate responsibility for both the origin and day-to-day functioning of other aspects of the universe God created, even while affirming the reality of secondary causes. . . .

It does seem theologically plausible, then, to hold that personhood emerges from the (physical) interaction of neurons in the brain. Such a view is consistent both with the holistic tenor of Scripture and with empirical evidence for continuity among living creatures and for mind-brain interdependence. If this is the case, then there would not seem to be—in principle—a *theological* reason why personhood could not emerge in similar fashion from the operation of a sufficiently complex technological artifact. (This, of course, is not the same as saying that such an accomplishment is technically possible, or, if so, when it might occur.)

Artificial Intelligence, Human Worth, and the Image of God

Should achievements in artificial intelligence [AI] impact our worth as persons? Historically, even before the era of computers, whenever a technological artifact has been able to surpass humans, people have seen this as a challenge to human worth. Today, when computers routinely out-perform humans in many tasks, people often take comfort in the fact that a computer is "only a machine." For example, after losing to Deep Blue [a chess-playing computer] in 1997, [chess grandmaster] Gary Kasparov was "rather gleeful that despite its win, it did not enjoy winning or gain any satisfaction from it." What if an artifact were to exist that made this comfort ring hollow?

An answer to this question hinges on how we understand the relationship between human worth, on the one hand, and a belief that the human constitution is fundamentally unique, on the other hand. When human worth is tied to human constitutional uniqueness, the possibility of strong AI [that is of an artificial intelligence that has human-like consciousness] seems to pose a serious threat to one of our most cherished concepts. Indeed, some have argued that developments in this area constitute the final blow to the notion of human specialness. First, they claim, [Polish astronomer Nicolaus] Copernicus and those who followed showed that our physical place in the universe is not special; then, [English naturalist Charles] Darwin and those who followed showed that our physical bodies are not special; finally, discoveries concerning animal intelligence along with artificial intelligence are showing that even our minds are not truly special. There are several possible responses to this.

One possible response is a form of denial: humans are special, and, therefore, whatever challenges this cannot possibly be true. At this point in time, actual achievements in the realm of artificial intelligence appear to leave that possibility open. . . . But it is not at all clear that this is a viable position in the long run. Moreover, even without artificial intelligence, study of animal behavior has shown that some (limited) aspects of intelligence, consciousness, and emotion may also be present in nonhuman animals.

A second possible response is to accept the data as implying that humans are actually not special. Instead, we are simply biological machines, and the fact that we are rational and conscious and have emotions constitutes a proof that machines can be rational, etc.—because we are. Living consistently with this perspective, however, is easier said than done. Some who are committed to the possibility of artificial persons deal with this by compartmentalizing their scientific and personal lives. For example, [robotics expert] Rodney Brooks wrote:

> On the one hand, I believe myself and my children all to be machines. Automatons at large in the universe. Every person I meet is also a machine—a bag of biochemicals interacting according to describable and knowable rules. When I look at my children I can, when I force myself, understand them in this way. I can see that they are machines interacting with the world. But this is not how I treat them. I treat them in a very special way, and I interact with them on an entirely different level. They have my unconditional love, the furthest

one might be able to get from rational analysis. Like a religious scientist, I maintain two sets of inconsistent beliefs and act on each of them in different circumstances.

A third possibility, however, is to recognize that constitutional uniqueness and value are really two very different things. That is, the proposition "if humans are not somehow constitutionally unique, then they don't have worth" is not actually a true statement. The account in Gen. 2:7 describes God as involved in a very intimate way with the origin of humanity—no other creature is it said that "God breathed into [its] nostrils the breath of life." Only after creating man and woman did God pronounce that his creation was not just good, but "very good." We naturally look for something in the way we are made that answers the question of why God values us. However, the same language used in Gen. 2:7 is also used with regard to animals elsewhere in Genesis, and biologically, humans are very similar to other organisms, even at the DNA level. Many writers feel (and I concur), that human worth has more to do with our *purpose* (our relationship to God and what God intends us to *be* and *do*), rather than our constitution (what we *are*). Our constitution is not what makes us special; rather, it is necessary so that we can be special. . . .

If, in the end, our value to God is not based on anything intrinsic to us, then the fear that artificial persons might somehow undermine our value as humans really represents a fundamental misunderstanding of biblical teaching. Of course, this also means that our worth as human beings cannot be understood without reference to our Creator. The existence of artificial persons might seriously undermine attempts to ground human worth in our intrinsic nature, apart from our value to God. But is this a bad thing? Perhaps technology, while seeming at times to lessen our need to depend on God, actually is having the opposite effect of showing us just how much we need him for our ultimate worth and purpose. Thus, though a secular form of humanism might indeed be threatened by the notion of artificial intelligence, a Christian form should not be.

Implications of a Biblical View of Personhood for Work in Artificial Intelligence

What ramifications, if any, does a biblical understanding of personhood have for work in artificial intelligence? Were it the case that there were a *theological* conflict between biblical teaching and the notion of strong AI or that strong AI were to constitute a threat to humanity's place in God's creation, then the answer might well be that Christians should confine their work to weak AI [that is, AI that does not match or exceed human capabilities] and steer clear of anything smacking of strong AI. This, of course, would raise the issue of where one draws the line. However, I have argued that neither of these is the case—i.e., there is no need to draw a *theological* line separating the doable from the not-doable (though the *ethical* ramifications of proposed applications would still need to be considered carefully). Given that no such line is called for, what does a biblical view of personhood have to say about work in artificial intelligence?

Much of the early work in artificial intelligence assumed that intelligence can be abstracted from implementation—what [philosopher] John Haugeland called GOFAI ("Good Old Fashioned Artificial Intelligence") or what others have called "symbolic AI." GOFAI claims that intelligence *is* symbolic computation; hence, it is possible, in principle, to implement intelligent processes (of "the same scope . . . as human action") in any sufficiently powerful physical symbol system, including, in particular, a human brain or a digital computer. Workers in symbolic AI have tended to focus on problems that require high-level human intelligence (e.g., playing chess, or expert performance in a domain such as medicine). While many such problems have yielded to this approach, everyday acts that we take for granted (e.g., distinguishing visually between a dog and a cat), or even things that "unintelligent" animals do routinely (e.g., moving around in a complex world), have proven intractable for symbolic AI.

In the past few decades, several other approaches have developed alongside symbolic AI. Connectionism (with roots that precede the digital computer) builds simulated neural networks that resemble the interconnection of the neurons in the brain. Genetic computing evolves programs using mechanisms modeled after biological evolution. Behavior-based robotics seeks to build systems that behave intelligently in the real world by directly coupling perception and action. Rodney Brooks, the originator of this approach, characterizes it in terms of two key ideas: "Situatedness: The robots are situated in the world, they do not deal with abstract descriptions" and "Embodiment: The robots have bodies and experience the world directly."

The Bible portrays humans as part of God's creation—the pinnacle of it, yes, but not in any sense, outside of it. In fact, Gen. 2:7 says that God formed us from the "dust of the ground," and the Bible sometimes speaks of humans as "dust" (Gen. 3:19; Ps. 103:14). God did not create abstract intelligence—he created physical brains, evidently using an evolutionary process, which incorporates features that closely resemble those in the brains of lower creatures. Approaches such as connectionism, genetic computing, and behavior-based robotics seem more in line with this than symbolic AI's view of intelligence as something abstract. (In fact, the latter more closely resembles Platonic dualism than biblical holism.) This is not at all to minimize the value of symbolic AI techniques for weak AI problems that have a strong symbolic component—often ones involving "higher" intelligence such as symbolic mathematics, "expert systems," natural language processing, or games like chess. But, in many areas, principles like those espoused by Brooks appear to be a better match to the biblical concept of personhood.

Moving beyond our origin, Genesis 3 makes it clear that we are not as God created us to be, and that death is a consequence of our sin. Genesis 3:15 introduces—and the rest of Scripture describes—God's plan for our redemption and restoration to eternal fellowship with him. It is possible, however, for work in artificial intelligence to be seen as an alternative to the hope revealed in Scripture. Hans Moravec and Ray Kurzweil, for example, contend that the very near future will see intelligent machines whose mental powers vastly exceed those of biological humans, and whose powers will allow the solving of problems that have long plagued humanity. Their works portray what amounts to an anticipated technological deliverance for the human race through what Moravec calls our "mind children." But Scripture insistently warns against idolatry, which basically involves looking to someone/thing other than our Creator to meet one's needs. Isaiah rightly mocks those who look to the works of their own hands to save them (Isa. 44:16–20). Would super-intelligent computers produced by our own hands really be the ultimate answer to the problems of humanity? Human history certainly suggests otherwise! Moreover, Moravec and Kurzweil argue that robotic technology might endow us with personal immortality. Here the goal is not so much to produce independent intelligences as to produce virtual brains into which a human's personality can be "uploaded," which, in conjunction with making backup copies periodically, will render a person immune to death by accident, disease, or old age. In contrast, the closing verses of Genesis 3 portray fallen man as being driven out of the Garden of Eden, because "He must not be allowed to reach out his hand and take from the tree of life and eat, and live forever" (Gen. 3:22). This is ultimately for our good, since an eternity in our fallen condition would quite literally be hell. (It is worth noting that, though Moravec and Kurzweil are highly respected and prolific researchers, their views are hardly representative of the mainstream of the AI community.)

As is true throughout the sciences, work in artificial intelligence can be wrongly motivated, but it can also represent a very legitimate part of humanity's fulfillment of the cultural mandate (Gen. 1:28) through enhanced understanding of the greatest marvel of God's creation: human beings. There is no inherent theological conflict between a biblical view of personhood and work in artificial intelligence, nor would successes in this field undermine human value or the doctrine of the image of God. This having been said, a realistic assessment of what has been accomplished to date suggests avoiding grandiose projections of what will be achieved in the near future (a temptation to which workers in this field have often yielded). We need to approach this area with an attitude of great caution and even reverence, for, as Scripture says, we are "fearfully and wonderfully made" (Ps. 139:14).

| "I am inclined to conclude that whatever is unique to humanity . . . is other than what computers do."

Christianity Suggests Limits to Artificial Intelligence

Harry Plantinga

Harry Plantinga is a professor in the computer science department at Calvin College in Michigan. In the following viewpoint, he argues that faith affects the way in which Christian computer scientists approach their work. He says that faith can lead Christian computer scientists to the recognition that the soul, rather than material computational abilities, separate human beings from machines. He also says faith affects the ethical choices made by Christian scientists.

As you read, consider the following questions:

1. What does Plantinga say follows for computer scientists who subscribe to the Christian belief that creation is real?

2. Describe how Plantinga says his Christian beliefs affected his response to the promises of the Lazarus Foundation?

Harry Plantinga, "Christianity and Computer Science at Calvin College," Calvin College—Computer Science. Reprinted with permission.

3. According to Plantinga, computers may be changing the way people think in what ways?

Computer science is a discipline with two aspects. On the one side it is an *engineering* discipline: it involves the planning, design, construction, and maintenance of computer systems. Its subject matter is corpus of techniques for analyzing problems, constructing solutions that won't collapse, guaranteeing and measuring the robustness of programs. (It is an *immature* engineering discipline, one realizes, when Microsoft Windows crashes yet again.)

Computer Science and God's Creation

On the other hand, I believe that it is also a *science* in the sense that mathematics is a science. It is the study of computation and computability, the study of *algorithm*. It does not frequently use the hypothesis-test method of studying nature, but it does involve the study of nature, in my opinion. The discovery of an aesthetically pleasing algorithmic solution to a difficult problem, the elucidation of the properties of the algorithm—these are ways of learning about God's creation. The world is created in such a way that certain problems have efficient solutions and other problems have no algorithmic solution at all. In fact, there is a rich structure to algorithmic complexity. Computer *science* investigates this structure.

In this scientific approach to the discipline, as we learn about God's creation, we also learn about God. We see something of the infinite riches of his wisdom and knowledge, his grace of hidden riches provided for humanity, his beauty. The appropriate attitude of the computer scientist is *doxology* [praises to God]. It is wonderful that any computable function can be embodied with a combination of two basic types of logic gates or that simple motions of rods and levers or rebounds of billiard balls can in principle play chess or factor a large number.

Our belief that creation is *real* and has a certain, fixed nature affects our approach to the discipline. We admit that there may be limits on computability and complexity of problems. We are willing to believe proofs regarding these matters. Yet because creation is fallen, we do not expect to find unadulterated perfection in computing. Even if a simple computer program were proven correct, we would allow for the possibility of hardware failure or a misunderstanding of the original problem. We take appropriate precautions and do not entrust too much to computers. We acknowledge that there will often be harmful as well as beneficial effects in the computerized solution of a problem.

The Nature of Humanity

There are also foundational issues in computer science in which a reformed, Christian perspective may affect research and teaching. One issue that interests me is the relationship between computing and thought. Our beliefs about the nature of humanity may affect our expectations about the future possibilities for artificial intelligence. On the other hand, the discoveries of artificial intelligence may help us improve our understanding of the nature of humanity.

In his *Institutes*, [John] Calvin [a Protestant thinker] strongly affirms that though the soul has organic faculties, it is *immortal* and *separable from the body*. He argues that human ability to reason, perform scientific investigation, invent "marvelous devices," even "divine the future—all while man sleeps" are "unfailing signs of divinity in man." Yet in a day when computers prove theorems and play chess, it . . . appears that some of the kinds of rationality Calvin had in mind are in fact *mechanizable*. Since finding regularities in the world, devising ingenious solutions to problems, and proving theorems can be performed by purely mechanical means . . . it is necessary (and possible) to define more closely what may be "unfailing signs of divinity in man."

[Thomas] Aquinas [a theologian and philosopher] places the intellect in the higher powers of the soul and memory and reason as parts of the intellect. Today, one would have to make more distinctions. Memory and reason—in the sense that computers have memory and can reason—are now known to be physical processes.

A conclusion some draw is that rationality is not, after all, unique to humans. Even *machines* can be rational. They have already been shown to be able to perform many tasks requiring rationality; there is no reason to think that others will not succumb eventually. If there is anything unique about humanity, it is not reason.

However, other conclusions are possible. I am inclined to conclude that whatever is unique to humanity, an "unfailing sign of divinity," is other than what computers do. Theorem proving, playing chess, and other forms of symbol manipulation according to rules are not uniquely human activities; after all, they can be performed by a machine. The rational soul is not unique it its computational and logical abilities, but in some other capabilities, such as those for intent, love, choice, and knowing God. If there is an aspect of memory and reason unique to the human intellect, it would have to be located in the meaning associated with the memory and reason.

In such discussions about the nature of personhood, presuppositions affect the range of conclusions that can be admitted. The materialist is limited in the possible ways of understanding humanity. Since she believes that all is material, she concludes that people are material objects, subject to physical laws. She is inclined to accept without proof the idea that any sort of "thinking" a person can do can be simulated by computer. And since the brain and the machine use different but functionally equivalent computational processes, the machine can think in the same sense as the brain.

Christians, who are not bound by the presupposition of materialism, are free to consider other possibilities, such as that God exists and is not a material object, that God is capable of working outside of physical law, and the traditional Christian view that people have an immortal, non-physical, separable soul, immediately created by God, endowed with the supernatural capabilities of love, will, and knowing God. Yet only the bravest or most foolhardy among us will claim to understand the nature of humanity and the union of humanity with the image of God. The Incarnation is after all one of the greatest acts of God and one of the greatest mysteries of the faith.

Foundational issues such as this one affect not only the theories we are willing to consider but the research programs we take on and even our hopes for eternal life. I recently received e-mail from the "Lazarus Foundation," which is attempting to set up an organization to research the making of backups of "brain programs." The idea is that in the event of major system failure (e.g. a plane crash or heart attack) the most recent brain program backup could be installed on alternate "wetware," perhaps a cloned body, thereby achieving eternal life. But I haven't yet met a Christian whose hope for eternal life is in having his brain program ported to another system. Even Christians who believe that people are material objects apparently don't limit the soul to a "brain program," a set of symbols appropriately manipulated. Our future is a new resurrection body and a new heavens and earth.

Computers and Ethics

The perspectival issues that arise in the engineering part of the discipline include motivation for work and choice of work area, professional responsibility, and ethics. We are in the image of a creative God, and we also love to create. There is a joy in creating something beautiful and useful out of the raw material that God provides. Love for God and neighbor is expressed in creating systems that solve problems, meet needs, and build up the church. And a unique power of this tool is

There Is a Spiritual Aspect to Intelligence

The body can be compared to the computer as both are machines. Both machines (the body and the computer) require intelligent direction from a spiritual living entity to function properly. I can think, I can reason, I can analyze the data and come to logical conclusions. Even if I program this into the computer, the computer just plays back my instructions. . . .

As you can never actually teach a tape recorder to speak you can also never teach a computer to think. The thinking is not done by the machine the thinking is done by the spiritual living entity present within the body.

Madhudvisa Dasa, "Artificial Intelligence—Getting Computers to Think," krisna.org, December 28, 2009. http://krisna.org.

that programs can be copied at almost no cost. Serving millions of people is as easy as serving one.

Professional responsibility and ethics are not only found among Christian computer engineers. The ACM [Association for Computing Machinery], the professional organization for computer scientists and engineers, publishes a code of professional responsibilities and ethics, to which ACM members voluntarily subscribe. However, the motivation for subscribing to ethical standards among Christians is different and perhaps stronger. The professional may find more reason to go out of her way to serve well when motivated by gratitude to God.

Finally, there are legion social issues that arise from the ubiquity of computing and computer-mediated communication. Computerization has transformed society in many ways. It has transformed our electronic and mechanical devices, our workplaces and types of work, our communication, and our recreation and leisure. We enjoy our sedentary communication and our recreation consisting in reading e-mail, browsing the web, and chatting on-line, but obesity is bursting out at the national seams. We enjoy the convenience of on-line purchasing, instant messaging, and electronic funds transfers, but our personal information, preferences, and finances are ever more closely tracked. We favor digital music, electronic books, and satellite TV, without accounting for the loss of the advantages of the physical artifact and the loss of consumer rights encrypted in electronic delivery. We e-mail and chat with our friends on-line, but we don't often consider the earthy fellowship and shared lives lost in such 'cyber society.'

Some are even suggesting that computers and electronic media are changing the way people think. Several sources of sound, images, and messages available at once combined with homework or computer games seem to be a common state for modern youth. Are we losing the ability to concentrate on a single subject, reason logically, and carry on a linear chain of reasoning? These are issues for cultural discernment from a Christian perspective.

As Christian computer scientists and engineers, we approach the study of our discipline in an attitude of doxology and service. We praise God as we study nature, and in gratitude we serve others. We are careful to honor God in what we do, and we find that in loving God we love others and in serving others we serve God. We choose the problems we will address through of a motivation of service, and we do our best to make our systems reliable, easy to use, and helpful, to honor God. We consider the social implications of our work and do our best to spur the beneficial aspects of computing. And in our service we find joy.

> *"Historically, all four approaches to AI [artificial intelligence] have been followed. . . . A human-centered approach must be in part an empirical science, involving observations and hypotheses about human behavior. A rationalist approach involves a combination of mathematics and engineering."*

The Possibility of Artificial Intelligence Depends on How Intelligence Is Defined

Stuart J. Russell and Peter Norvig

Stuart J. Russell is a professor of computer science at the University of California at Berkeley; Peter Norvig is director of research at Google, Inc. In the following viewpoint, they argue that artificial intelligence (AI) has a number of definitions. They say computers can be considered to have achieved AI when they act like humans, when they think like humans, when they think rationally, or when they act rationally. They conclude that each of these approaches to AI has advantages and limitations.

Stuart J. Russell and Peter Norvig, "Introduction," *Artificial Intelligence: A Modern Approach*, 3rd ed., Prentice Hall, 2010, pp. 1–5. Reprinted with permission.

As you read, consider the following questions:

1. What four capabilities would a computer need to pass a regular Turing test, according to the authors?

2. What do the authors say we must do if we are going to say that a given program thinks like a human?

3. According to the authors, what is one way we act rationally without relying on inference?

In [this viewpoint's insert] we see eight definitions of AI [artificial intelligence], laid out along two dimensions. The definitions on top are concerned with *thought processes* and *reasoning*, whereas the ones on the bottom address *behavior*. The definitions on the left measure success in terms of fidelity to *human* performance, whereas the ones on the right measure against an *ideal* performance measure, called rationality. A system is rational if it does the "right thing," given what it knows.

Historically, all four approaches to AI have been followed, each by different people with different methods. A human-centered approach must be in part an empirical science, involving observations and hypotheses about human behavior. A rationalist approach involves a combination of mathematics and engineering. The various groups have both disparaged and helped each other. Let us look at the four approaches in more detail.

Acting Humanly: The Turing Test Approach

The *Turing Test*, proposed by Alan Turing (1950), was designed to provide a satisfactory operational definition of intelligence. A computer passes the test if a human interrogator, after posing some written questions, cannot tell whether the written responses come from a person or from a computer. . . .

Programming a computer to pass a rigorously applied test provides plenty to work on. The computer would need to possess the following capabilities:

- *natural language processing* to enable it to communicate successfully in English;

- *knowledge representation* to store what it knows or hears;

- *automated reasoning* to use the stored information to answer questions and to draw new conclusions;

- *machine learning* to adapt to new circumstances and to detect and extrapolate patterns.

Turing's test deliberately avoided direct physical interaction between the interrogator and the computer, because *physical* simulation of a person is unnecessary for intelligence. However, the so-called *total Turing Test* includes a video signal so that the interrogator can test the subject's perceptual abilities, as well as the opportunity for the interrogator to pass physical objects "through the hatch." To pass the total Turing Test, the computer will need

- *computer vision* to perceive objects, and

- *robotics* to manipulate objects and move about.

These six disciplines compose most of AI, and Turing deserves credit for designing a test that remains relevant 60 years later. Yet AI researchers have devoted little effort to passing the Turing Test, believing that it is more important to study the underlying principles of intelligence than to duplicate an exemplar. The quest for "artificial flight" succeeded when the Wright brothers and others stopped imitating birds and started using wind tunnels and learning about aerodynamics. Aeronautical engineering texts do not define the goal of their field as making "machines that fly so exactly like pigeons that they can fool even other pigeons."

Thinking Humanly: The Cognitive Modeling Approach

If we are going to say that a given program thinks like a human, we must have some way of determining how humans think. We need to get *inside* the actual workings of human minds. There are three ways to do this: through introspection—trying to catch our own thoughts as they go by; through psychological experiments—observing a person in action; and through brain imaging—observing the brain in action. Once we have a sufficiently precise theory of the mind, it becomes possible to express the theory as a computer program. If the program's input-output behavior matches corresponding human behavior, that is evidence that some of the program's mechanisms could also be operating in humans. For example, Allen Newell and Herbert Simon, who developed GPS, the "General Problem Solver", were not content merely to have their program solve problems correctly. They were more concerned with comparing the trace of its reasoning steps to traces of human subjects solving the same problems. The interdisciplinary field of *cognitive science* brings together computer models from AI and experimental techniques from psychology to construct precise and testable theories of the human mind. . . .

We will occasionally comment on similarities or differences between AI techniques and human cognition. Real cognitive science, however, is necessarily based on experimental investigation of actual humans or animals. . . .

In the early days of AI there was often confusion between the approaches: an author would argue that an algorithm performs well on a task and that it is *therefore* a good model of human performance, or vice versa. Modern authors separate the two kinds of claims; this distinction has allowed both AI and cognitive science to develop more rapidly. The two fields continue to fertilize each other, most notably in computer vision, which incorporates neurophysiological evidence into computational models.

Thinking Rationally: The "Laws of Thought" Approach

The Greek philosopher Aristotle was one of the first to attempt to codify "right thinking," that is, irrefutable reasoning processes. His *syllogisms* provided patterns for argument structures that always yielded correct conclusions when given correct premises—for example, "Socrates is a man; all men are mortal; therefore, Socrates is mortal." These laws of thought were supposed to govern the operation of the mind; their study initiated the field called *logic.*

Logicians in the 19th century developed a precise notation for statements about all kinds of objects in the world and the relations among them. (Contrast this with ordinary arithmetic notation, which provides only for statements about *numbers.*) By 1965, programs existed that could, in principle, solve *any* solvable problem described in logical notation. (Although if no solution exists, the program might loop forever.) The so-called *logicist* tradition within artificial intelligence hopes to build on such programs to create intelligent systems.

There are two main obstacles to this approach. First, it is not easy to take informal knowledge and state it in the formal terms required by logical notation, particularly when the knowledge is less than 100% certain. Second, there is a big difference between solving a problem "in principle" and solving it in practice. Even problems with just a few hundred facts can exhaust the computational resources of any computer unless it has some guidance as to which reasoning steps to try first. Although both of these obstacles apply to *any* attempt to build computational reasoning systems, they appeared first in the logicist tradition.

Definitions of Artificial Intelligence	
Thinking Humanly "The exciting new effort to make computers think . . . *machines with minds*, in the full and literal sense." (Haugeland, 1985) "[The automation of] activities that we associate with human thinking, activities such as decision-making, problem solving, learning . . ." (Bellman, 1978)	***Thinking Rationally*** "The study of mental faculties through the use of computational models." (Charniak and McDermott, 1985) "The study of the computations that make it possible to perceive, reason, and act." (Winston, 1992)
Acting Humanly "The art of creating machines that perform functions that require intelligence when performed by people." (Kurzweil, 1990) "The study of how to make computers do things at which, at the moment, people are better." (Rich and Knight, 1991)	***Acting Rationally*** "Computational Intelligence is the study of the design of intelligent agents." (Poole *et al.*, 1998) "AI . . . is concerned with intelligent behavior in artifacts." (Nilsson, 1998)

TAKEN FROM: Stuart J. Russell and Peter Norvig, *Artificial Intelligence: A Modern Approach*, 3rd ed., Upper Saddle River, NJ: Prentice Hall, 2010.

Acting Rationally: The Rational Agent Approach

An *agent* is just something that acts (*agent* comes from the Latin *agere*, to do). Of course, all computer programs do something, but computer agents are expected to do more: operate autonomously, perceive their environment, persist over a prolonged time period, adapt to change, and create and pursue goals. A *rational agent* is one that acts so as to achieve the best outcome or, when there is uncertainty, the best expected outcome.

In the "laws of thought" approach to AI, the emphasis was on correct inferences. Making correct inferences is sometimes *part* of being a rational agent, because one way to act rationally is to reason logically to the conclusion that a given action will achieve one's goals and then to act on that conclusion. On the other hand, correct inference is not *all* of rationality; in some situations, there is no provably correct thing to do, but something must still be done. There are also ways of acting rationally that cannot be said to involve inference. For example, recoiling from a hot stove is a reflex action that is usually more successful than a slower action taken after careful deliberation.

All the skills needed for the Turing Test also allow an agent to act rationally. Knowledge representation and reasoning enable agents to reach good decisions. We need to be able to generate comprehensible sentences in natural language to get by in a complex society. We need learning not only for erudition, but also because it improves our ability to generate effective behavior.

The rational-agent approach has two advantages over the other approaches. First, it is more general than the "laws of thought" approach because correct inference is just one of several possible mechanisms for achieving rationality. Second, it is more amenable to scientific development than are approaches based on human behavior or human thought. The standard of rationality is mathematically well defined and completely general, and can be "unpacked" to generate agent designs that provably achieve it. Human behavior, on the other hand, is well adapted for one specific environment and is defined by, well, the sum total of all the things that humans do. . . .

One important point to keep in mind: . . . achieving perfect rationality—always doing the right thing—is not feasible in complicated environments. The computational demands are just too high. . . . However, . . . perfect rationality is a good starting point for analysis. It simplifies the problem and provides the appropriate setting for most of the foundational material in the field.

> *"The search for artificial intelligence [AI] modelled on human brains has been a dismal failure. AI based on ant behaviour, though, is having some success."*

Artificial Intelligence Based on Insects Seems Possible Soon

The Economist

The Economist is a British business and news magazine. In the following viewpoint, the author argues that insect swarm activity may be a more promising model for artificial intelligence (AI) than human intelligence. For example, the viewpoint says that AI programmers have studied the way that ant colonies find food by laying down pheromones. This has led to the development of software that has been useful for delivery firms planning out routes. The viewpoint also suggests that the way that insect swarms reach decisions may be similar to the way that neurons interact in the human brain.

As you read, consider the following questions:

1. What is the traveling salesman problem, and how do ants solve their version of it, according to this viewpoint?

The Economist, "Artificial Intelligence: Riders on a Swarm," August 12, 2010. Reprinted with permission.

2. What is AntNet, according to the viewpoint?

3. According to *The Economist*, what is a waggle dance, and how do bees use it in selecting nesting sites?

One of the bugaboos that authors of science fiction sometimes use to scare their human readers is the idea that ants may develop intelligence and take over the Earth. The purposeful collective activity of ants and other social insects does, indeed, look intelligent on the surface. An illusion, presumably. But it might be a good enough illusion for computer scientists to exploit. The search for artificial intelligence modelled on human brains has been a dismal failure. AI based on ant behaviour, though, is having some success.

Ants first captured the attention of software engineers in the early 1990s. A single ant cannot do much on its own, but the colony as a whole solves complex problems such as building a sophisticated nest, maintaining it, and filling it with food. That rung a bell with people like Marco Dorigo, who is now a researcher at the Free University of Brussels and was one of the founders of a field that has become known as swarm intelligence.

In particular, Dr Dorigo was interested to learn that ants are good at choosing the shortest possible route between a food source and their nest. This is reminiscent of a classic computational conundrum, the travelling-salesman problem. Given a list of cities and their distances apart, the salesman must find the shortest route needed to visit each city once. As the number of cities grows, the problem gets more complicated. A computer trying to solve it will take longer and longer, and suck in more and more processing power. The reason the travelling-salesman problem is so interesting is that many other complex problems, including designing silicon chips and assembling DNA sequences, ultimately come down to a modified version of it.

Ants solve their own version using chemical signals called pheromones. When an ant finds food, she takes it back to the nest, leaving behind a pheromone trail that will attract others. The more ants that follow the trail, the stronger it becomes. The pheromones evaporate quickly, however, so once all the food has been collected, the trail soon goes cold. Moreover, this rapid evaporation means long trails are less attractive than short ones, all else being equal. Pheromones thus amplify the limited intelligence of the individual ants into something more powerful.

Hivemind

In 1992 Dr Dorigo and his group began developing Ant Colony Optimisation (ACO), an algorithm that looks for solutions to a problem by simulating a group of ants wandering over an area and laying down pheromones. ACO proved good at solving travelling-salesman-type problems. Since then it has grown into a whole family of algorithms, which have been applied to many practical questions.

Its most successful application is in logistics. Migros, a Swiss supermarket chain, and Barilla, Italy's leading pasta-maker, both manage their daily deliveries from central warehouses to local retailers using AntRoute. This is a piece of software developed by AntOptima, a spin-off from the Dalle Molle Institute for Artificial Intelligence in Lugano (IDSIA), one of Europe's leading centres for swarm intelligence. Every morning the software's "ants" calculate the best routes and delivery sequences, depending on the quantity of cargo, its destinations, delivery windows and available lorries. According to Luca Gambardella, the director of both IDSIA and AntOptima, it takes 15 minutes to produce a delivery plan for 1,200 trucks, even though the plan changes almost every day.

Ant-like algorithms have also been applied to the problem of routing information through communication networks. Dr Dorigo and Gianni Di Caro, another researcher at IDSIA, have developed AntNet, a routing protocol in which packets of information hop from node to node, leaving a trace that signals the "quality" of their trip as they do so. Other packets sniff the trails thus created and choose accordingly. In computer simulations and tests on small-scale networks, AntNet has been shown to outperform existing routing protocols. It is better able to adapt to changed conditions (for example, increased traffic) and has a more robust resistance to node failures. According to Dr Di Caro, many large companies in the routing business have shown interest in AntNet, but using it would require the replacement of existing hardware, at huge cost. Ant routing looks promising, however, for *ad hoc* mobile networks like those used by the armed forces and civil-protection agencies.

Routing, of both bytes and lorries, is what mathematicians call a discrete problem, with a fixed, albeit large, number of solutions. For continuous problems, with a potentially infinite number of solutions—such as finding the best shape for an aeroplane wing—another type of swarm intelligence works better. Particle swarm optimisation (PSO), which was invented by James Kennedy and Russell Eberhart in the mid 1990s, is inspired more by birds than by insects. When you place a bird feeder on your balcony, it may take some time for the first bird to find it, but from that moment many others will soon flock around. PSO algorithms try to recreate this effect. Artificial birds fly around randomly, but keep an eye on the others and always follow the one that is closest to "food". There are now about 650 tested applications of PSO, ranging from image and video analysis to antenna design, from diagnostic systems in medicine to fault detection in industrial machines.

Digital ants and birds, then, are good at thinking up solutions to problems, but Dr Dorigo is now working on something that can act as well as think: robots. A swarm of small, cheap robots can achieve through co-operation the same results as individual big, expensive robots—and with more flex-

"This is my brother Dave. He's real smart—brain the size of a pea!" cartoon by Tim Cordell, wwwCartoonStock.com. Copyright © Tim Cordell. Reproduction rights obtainable from www.CartoonStock.com.

ibility and robustness; if one robot goes down, the swarm keeps going. Later this summer, he will be ready to demonstrate his "Swarmanoid" project. This is based on three sorts of small, simple robots, each with a different function, that co-operate in exploring an environment. Eye-bots take a look around and locate interesting objects. Foot-bots then give hand-bots a ride to places identified by the eye-bots. The hand-bots pick up the objects of interest. And they all run home.

All this is done without any pre-existing plan or central co-ordination. It relies on interactions between individual robots. According to Dr Dorigo, bot-swarms like this could be used for surveillance and rescue—for example, locating survivors and retrieving valuable goods during a fire.

Intellidance

Swarmanoid robots may not much resemble the creatures that originally inspired the field, but insects continue to give programmers ideas. Dr Dorigo's group has, for instance, developed a system to allow robots to detect when a swarm member is malfunctioning. This was inspired by the way some fireflies synchronise their light emissions so that entire trees flash on and off. The robots do the same, and if one light goes out of synch because of a malfunction the other bots can react quickly, either isolating the maverick so that it cannot cause trouble, or calling back to base to have it withdrawn.

All of which is encouraging. But anyone who is really interested in the question of artificial intelligence cannot help but go back to the human mind and wonder what is going on there—and there are those who think that, far from being an illusion of intelligence, what Dr Dorigo and his fellows have stumbled across may be a good analogue of the process that underlies the real thing.

For example, according to Vito Trianni of the Institute of Cognitive Sciences and Technologies, in Rome, the way bees select nesting sites is strikingly like what happens in the brain. Scout bees explore an area in search of suitable sites. When they discover a good location, they return to the nest and perform a waggle dance (similar to the one used to indicate patches of nectar-rich flowers) to recruit other scouts. The higher the perceived quality of the site, the longer the dance and the stronger the recruitment, until enough scouts have been recruited and the rest of the swarm follows. Substitute nerve cells for bees and electric activity for waggle dances, and you have a good description of what happens when a stimulus produces a response in the brain.

Proponents of so-called swarm cognition, like Dr Trianni, think the brain might work like a swarm of nerve cells, with no top-down co-ordination. Even complex cognitive functions, such as abstract reasoning and consciousness, they suggest, might simply emerge from local interactions of nerve cells doing their waggle dances. Those who speak of intellectual buzz, then, might be using a metaphor which is more apt than they realise.

Periodical and Internet Sources Bibliography

The following articles have been selected to supplement the diverse views presented in this chapter.

Jonathan Fildes	"Artificial Brain '10 Years Away,'" *BBC News*, July 22, 2009.
David Gelernter	"Artificial Intelligence Is Lost in the Woods," *Technology Review*, July 2007.
Ben Goertzel, Seth Baum, and Ted Goertzel	"How Long Till Human-Level AI?" *h+ Magazine*, February 5, 2010.
John Horgan	"Brain Chips and Other Dreams of the Cyber-Evangelists," *Chronicle of Higher Education*, June 3, 2005.
Ray Kurzweil	"Ray Kurzweil on the Singularity," *Non-Prophet*, January 2006.
———	"Ray Kurzweil Responds to 'Ray Kurzweil Does Not Understand the Brain,'" www.kurzweilAI.net, August 20, 2010.
John Markoff	"The Coming Superbrain," *New York Times*, May 23, 2009.
John McCarthy	"What Is Artificial Intelligence?," www.stanford.edu, November 12, 2007.
PZ Myers	"Ray Kurzweil Does Not Understand the Brain," *Pharyngula*, August 17, 2010.
Doug Wolens	"Singularity 101 with Vernor Vinge," *h+ Magazine*, April 22, 2009.

CHAPTER 2

What Does the Turing Test Reveal About Artificial Intelligence?

Chapter Preface

A lan Turing was an English mathematician and computer scientist. He was one of the most important scientists in the founding of research into computers and artificial intelligence.

Turing was born in 1912. He struggled in school because his interests in unusual mathematical problems and ideas distracted him from the prescribed curriculum. However, eventually his intelligence was recognized, and he went to the University of Cambridge to study mathematics.

At Cambridge, he wrote his first seminal paper, "On Computable Numbers with an Application to the Entscheidungsproblem." This paper led to the idea of a Turing machine—an actual mechanism that could be instructed to solve a particular problem or series of problems. The Turing machine became the conceptual basis for the modern computer, "a single machine which can be turned to any well-defined task by being supplied with the appropriate program," as Andrew Hodges described it on www.turing.org.uk.

Turing went on to work on artificial intelligence and calculating machines. His innovations in this area made him a vital part of the British team that worked on decoding the Nazi Enigma code during World War II (1939–1945). "His so called 'bombe' machine was able to rapidly decode the 158 million, million, million variations used by the Nazis in their commands with the creation of a prototype high-speed processor. It saved tens of thousands of lives and variations on the original helped both the British and the US to eventual victory," according to Jonathan Brown in an August 18, 2009, article in *The Independent*.

Following the war, Turing continued his work in the field of artificial intelligence. However in 1952, he was arrested for having sex with another man, which was a crime at that time in Britain. The punishment included estrogen treatments, which made Turing "impotent and caused his breasts to grow," according to author Charles Petzold in a June 28, 2008, article on www.charlespetzold.com. Despite being a war hero, Turing's career options were seriously curtailed by his conviction. In 1954, at the age of 41, he committed suicide. It is generally thought that the humiliation of his prosecution led to his death.

The following viewpoints focus on one of Turing's best known ideas, the Turing Test, which established a method for determining whether a given computer program had attained artificial intelligence.

> "Turing's intelligence criterion is attrac-
> tive because the decision is based on
> purely observable, external characteris-
> tics. Thus, without having to know how
> intelligence arises ... we can ascertain
> its presence."

The Turing Test Is a Good Test of Artificial Intelligence

Virginia Savova and Leonid Peshkin

Virginia Savova is a postdoctoral associate at the Massachusetts Institute of Technology; Leonid Peshkin is a professor at Harvard University. In the following viewpoint, they argue that the Turing test is a valid test of artificial intelligence (AI). They contend that a machine could not fake its way through the Turing Test in a manner that violates our intuitions about intelligence. They also contend that no look-up table could be composed to allow a machine to adequately pass the Turing Test.

As you read, consider the following questions:

1. According to the viewpoint, why did Alan Turing himself express skepticism about the Turing Test?

Virginia Savova and Leonid Peshkin, "Is the Turing Test Good Enough? The Fallacy of Resource-Unbounded Intelligence," *Proceedings of the 20th International Joint Conference on Artificial Intelligence,* International Joint Conferences on Artificial Intelligence, 2007, pp. 545–550. Reprinted with permission.

2. What do the authors say is the problem with claiming that knowledge of the real world is central to intelligence?

3. Why do the authors say that a Turing Test of one second can be passed by any machine?

The poet James Whitcomb Riley (1849–1916) is often remembered for his formulation of the "duck criterion": "When I see a bird that walks like a duck and swims like a duck and quacks like a duck, I call that bird a duck."

Ducks and Machines

With a similarly practical attitude, many AI [artificial intelligence] researchers would say a machine that talks intelligently and behaves intelligently should be called intelligent. This assumption was formalized by Alan Turing who proposed a behavioral test for determining whether a machine can think. In its original formulation, the Turing test is an imitation game, in which a machine does its best to imitate a human participant in free flowing conversation with a judge. At the end of the game, the judge is asked to point out the human participant. If under repeated sessions of the game, the judge is at chance [that is, guesses the machine as often as the human], the machine should be considered intelligent.

It is fairly obvious that passing the Turing test is not a necessary condition of intelligence. For one, most humans have never been subjected to such a test. Furthermore, an intelligent agent might fail the test due to temporary impairments, such as being sleepy, hungry or on drugs. Finally, an intelligent machine might fail the Turing test because it may believe it is in its best interest not to show how intelligent it is.

Thus, the Turing test debate in the literature has centered around the question of whether the test represents a sufficient condition for intelligence. Turing himself is fairly unconvinced on this issue. His skepticism derives from the conclusion that the question of machine intelligence is very much alike the question of other minds. It is impossible, the solipsist argument goes, to know for sure whether there exist any other conscious beings apart from one's self, since one only has direct access to one's own consciousness. Thus, rather than directly arguing in favor of his test as a sufficient condition, he claims that the test is simply a good approximation to some true characteristic of intelligence, which is both currently unknown and impossible to observe.

But despite Turing's reluctance to adopt a strong stance, philosophers have taken this position seriously in both defending and disproving it, and for a good reason. In the absence of this strong assertion, the power of the Turing test as a diagnostic is severely limited, and its status is reduced to a dubious replacement for the true definition of intelligence. In other words, why would we take the Turing test more seriously than any other arbitrarily formulated criterion? Its only advantage appears to be that it would pick out all humans, who constitute—by assumption—the pool of known intelligent entities. However, we can achieve similar success by replacing the definition of intelligence with the definition of featherless biped. Countless other criteria would do the same, while having little to do with our intuition of what intelligence is as a trait. That is why it is important to figure out the extent to which Turing's criterion can be deemed sufficient for ascertaining intelligence.

Just like Riley's duck criterion, Turing's intelligence criterion is attractive because the decision is based on purely observable, external characteristics. Thus, without having to know how intelligence arises or what it is made of, we can ascertain its presence purely by observing its interactions with the environment. This gives rise to the foundational claim of AI and cognitive science—that intelligence can be understood and reproduced in an abstract computational device.

But the Turing test's most attractive aspect is precisely the one open for most criticism. Powerful objections have been raised to the effect that the definition of intelligence requires access to the inner workings of the computational mechanism used by the machine, rather than its behavior per se. The objections are illustrated by two famous thought experiments: Searle's Chinese Room and Block's Aunt Bertha.

The Chinese Room

[American Philosopher John] Searle imagines a monolingual English speaker locked in a room with Chinese symbols and a large set of instructions in English about mapping sequences of these symbols to other sequences. His interrogators outside come up with a Chinese story along with a set of questions about the story. They hand the story and the questions to the person inside the room, who then looks up the sequence of symbols in the instruction manual and produces what his interrogators might view as a reply. Despite performing adequately on the verbal Chinese test, the person inside the room does not understand Chinese. Instead, s/he merely appears to understand Chinese, i.e. simulates understanding of Chinese. Similarly, Searle argues, a machine can fake its way out of the Turing Test without satisfying our deep intuition of what it means to be truly intelligent.

Searle's thought experiment appears to conflate two issues, and it is worth teasing those apart. One issue is the issue of information content. The formal symbol stands for an entity in the real world. Obviously, any machine which has no access to the mapping from the formal symbol to the entity cannot be said to understand what the formal symbol means.

The other issue is the type of information storage and access. It is our intuition that there is something profoundly unintelligent about interacting with the environment through a look-up table, or by following an externally generated sequence of steps. The problem with this scenario is that the intelligence observed in the behavior of the agent originates outside of the agent, which is in and of itself incapable of generating novel behavior. This is the issue of generative incapacity. . . .

Hamburgers and Blindness

We take issue with Searle's assumption that meaning is central to our notion of intelligence. To clarify, let us suppose that locked in the Chinese room is a Chinese speaker, who by some accident of fate has never encountered a hamburger. The interrogators hand him a story involving hamburgers, and ask him questions, which s/he answers to the best of his/her abilities. When asked about properties of hamburgers that cannot be inferred from the story, s/he claims ignorance or makes a guess. Obviously, it would not be reasonable for us to claim that the Chinese speaker does not understand Chinese simply because s/he does not know the properties of hamburgers. If anything, we would say that s/he understands Chinese, but not the world of American diners.

Similarly, the fact that the machine does not understand what a formal symbol's relationship to the world does not necessarily imply that it should be labeled "unintelligent." Rather, the design limitation of the machine, its different embodiment and experience make it differ from a human in ways irrelevant to the question at hand, just as a Chinese person who has not been exposed to hamburgers differs from a American speaker of Chinese.

Of course, we could claim that knowledge of the real world is essential to human intelligence, and that anyone who exhibits verbal behavior without accompanying knowledge does not qualify as intelligence. However, such an assertion is controversial, and can hardly be held to form a central part of our common sense intuition. For example, we usually consider congenitally blind individuals to be just as intelligent as the rest of us, even though they are deprived from a certain type of knowledge of the real world. Their inability to relate visual-based concepts to the real world is an accident, and does not bear on their intrinsic intelligence. If we accept that blind (or deaf) individuals are intelligent, the question becomes, how much real world deprivation can an entity handle [and] still be considered intelligent. Would we be willing to set some arbitrary threshold, for example, such that blind people are intelligent, but deaf and blind people are not, or that deaf and blind people are intelligent, but deaf and blind people with no haptic sensation [sense of touch] are not? While imagining this gruesome scenario is difficult, it would help us understand Searle's objection.

Our intuition regarding the intelligence of individuals who lack any non-verbal stimulation is far from obvious. For example, what if a subject of a profoundly unethical cognitive science were raised confined to a bed, blindfolded and fed through an IV, but verbally taught to do mathematics? The question whether such a person is intelligent is difficult to answer, but the intuition is not as clear-cut as Searle would like us to believe.

Look-up Tables and Aunt Bertha

In addition to the symbol-grounding problem, Searle's thought experiment raises another issue: to what extent are the inner workings of the computing mechanism relevant to intelligence? The intuition that the Chinese room lacks intelligence is partially due to the absence of data compression and generalization in the symbol manipulation process.

Let us say that [there are] two Chinese impostors that differ only in the type of instruction manual they have committed to memory. The first impostor's manual lists all stories in Chinese of finite length, and all questions about them, in a giant lookup table. The second impostor on the other hand has memorized a much leaner manual, which instructs the person to analyze the questions and build answers in a combinatorial fashion. While we may be reluctant to say that either person understands what Chinese words mean, it is clear that the latter understands something about how Chinese works, which the former does not. Thus, our intuitions about the Chinese Room experiment also depend on the way in which—we are told—information is represented and accessed.

The concern is legitimate from the point of view of AI. While different people might have different intuitions regarding the contribution of real-world knowledge to intelligence, we believe that most AI researchers would find a look-up table approach to question-answering unintelligent. This intuition is best clarified by Ned Block in his Aunt Bertha argument.

Imagine that the length of the Turing test is known to us in advance, e.g. one hour. Now imagine that Block [has] a machine with extremely large storage capacity, and programs it to converse by looking up the answer to any question in a giant look-up table. This is possible, Block claims, because the number of questions that can be asked in a 1-hour Turing test is finite, and of finite length. He will construct the table by consulting an actual human—Aunt Bertha—on all possible conversations of some length 1. Obviously, the performance of the machine on the test would not constitute a proof of its intelligence—it would merely be a testimony to Aunt Bertha's intelligence. Hence, Block argues, passing the Turing test cannot be thought of as a sufficient condition for intelligence.

To use a different metaphor: one wouldn't want to administer the Turing test to a walkie-talkie, which is remotely tuned in to Aunt Bertha. Obviously, while the answers coming from the walkie-talkie are intelligent, it is not. Essentially, a machine that recorded the answers of Aunt Bertha is merely a mechanism for transmitting Aunt Bertha's intelligence, and does not itself possess intelligence.

What is missing in both cases is *information compression and generalization on the part of the device whose intelligence we are probing*. The Aunt Bertha machine can only respond to the questions for which it was programmed, and the answers to related questions are related only because they were so in the mind of Aunt Bertha. Despite this unintelligent organization of information however, the Aunt Bertha machine is claimed to be capable of passing the Turing test.

Thus, one option is to amend Turing's definition of intelligence as follows:

> If an agent has the capacity to produce a sensible sequence of verbal responses to a sequence of verbal stimuli, whatever they may be, and without requiring storage exponential in the length of the sequence, then it is intelligent [Stuart M.] Shieber, 2006].

The problem with the revised definition is that it is no longer purely behavioral, because it requires us to examine the internal workings of the candidate entity. Therefore, Block argues, the Turing test is not a sufficient condition of intelligence.

Why Block Is Wrong

We begin by attacking the . . . argument, . . . that it is possible to construct a look-up table which can definitely pass a non-trivial Turing test. By non-trivial we mean a test which is sufficiently long to allow the judge to conclude that a human possesses human intelligence.

To clarify, let us examine the notion of test length, and its influence on the argument. It is obvious that the shorter the test is, the easier it is for a machine to pass. In fact, if the test is sufficiently short, it will be passed by any machine. Suppose the test is as short as one second. No human would be able to say anything in one second, and neither would the machine. Hence, the judge would be at chance on a forced choice. Obviously, this type of failure of the Turing test is not a reason for eliminating it as a sufficient condition for the presence of intelligence. We tacitly assume that the Turing test has to be administered for a reasonable period of time.

This is the first step toward exposing the possibility-of-construction fallacy. We will show that Ned Block's argument relies on the unwarranted assumption that real-world time and space limitations are not a factor in the Turing test. Given that we accept—and we certainly have to—that the Turing test is only meaningful beyond some minimal length, it becomes an important question whether an appropriate look-up table can be constructed to pass it.

Let us review Ned Block's proposed way of constructing the Aunt Bertha machine. He suggests to exhaustively conduct with Aunt Bertha all conversations of length one hour. Presumably, Aunt Bertha would devote her lifetime to this process. But even if Aunt Bertha lives extraordinarily long, this is impossible. Suppose that Block somehow manages to record not only Aunt Bertha's one hour conversations, but all hour long conversations that took place since humans got the ability to speak. It is clear that even in this case, the look-up table would not contain all possible one hour conversations. This is because a) the set of possible conversations depends on the natural, social and cultural environment and evolves with it and b) because future conversations can always reference those conversations that have previously occurred. For example, while a conversation like:

-Have you heard the new Federline[1] rap song?

-Yes, I have it on my iPod.

is fairly common nowadays [2007], it would have been impossible just five years ago. Similarly, a conversation about [Greek philosopher] Plato's dialogues would have been impossible when Plato was five years old. Thus, while it is true that the set of all possible conversations of fixed length is finite at any given point in time, it is not true that it is the same set. Crucially, the set of all hourlong conversations would change from the time when Aunt Bertha's recordings would have ended to the time when the Turing test would begin.

1. Kevin Federline is a dancer and rapper.

In fairness, Block does anticipate this counter argument, but dismisses it on the grounds that the Turing test is not a test of knowledge, but of intelligence, and therefore ignorance of current events does not constitute grounds for failing:

> A system can be intelligent, yet have no knowledge of current events. Likewise, a machine can imitate intelligence without imitating knowledge of current events. The programmers could, if they liked, choose to simulate an intelligent Robinson Crusoe who knows nothing of the last twenty-five years.

However, Block's reply to this challenge is inadequate. While an intelligent system need not have knowledge of current events, it should be capable of learning about them and subsequently commenting on them in the context of the test. A machine which relies on a finite look-up table will not be able to accomplish this, because it is unable to add previously nonexisting entries.

| *"A computer that fools a fool is hardly proof of artificial intelligence."*

The Turing Test Cannot Prove Artificial Intelligence

Mark Halpern

Mark Halpern is a computer software expert who has worked at IBM. In the following viewpoint, he argues that the Turing Test is fundamentally flawed. As evidence, he points to Turing Tests conducted in 1991. During the Turing Tests, Halpern says, the judging was flagrantly inadequate; computers that were generating random nonsense were judged human, while some humans were judged to be computers. Halpern concludes that even if a computer were to pass the Turing Test, it would not show that that computer had achieved artificial intelligence.

As you read, consider the following questions:

1. Why did some judges mistake Cynthia Clay for a computer, according to Halpern?

2. How does Halpern suggest a judge could force a computer to respond to the ideas rather than to the words in a question?

Mark Halpern, "The Trouble with the Turing Test," *The New Atlantis 11*, Winter 2006. Reprinted with permission.

3. What does Halpern suggest we should do instead of accepting the possibility of thinking machines or sinking back into the Dark Ages?

Perhaps the absurdity of trying to make computers that can "think" is best demonstrated by reviewing a series of attempts to do just that—by aiming explicitly to pass Turing's test.[1] In 1991, a New Jersey businessman named Hugh Loebner founded and subsidized an annual competition, the Loebner Prize Competition in Artificial Intelligence, to identify and reward the computer program that best approximates artificial intelligence [AI] as Turing defined it. The first few Competitions were held in Boston under the auspices of the Cambridge Center for Behavioral Studies; since then they have been held in a variety of academic and semi-academic locations. But only the first, held in 1991, was well documented and widely reported on in the press, making that inaugural event our best case study.

Practical Problems

The officials presiding over the competition had to settle a number of details ignored in Turing's paper, such as how often the judges must guess that a computer is human before we accept their results as significant, and how long a judge may interact with a hidden entity before he has to decide. For the original competition, the host center settled such questions with arbitrary decisions—including the number of judges, the method of selecting them, and the instructions they were given.

Beyond these practical concerns, there are deeper questions about how to interpret the range of possible outcomes: What conclusions are we justified in reaching if the judges are generally successful in identifying humans as humans and

1. Alan Turing argued that a computer could be judged to have artificial intelligence if a human having a conversation with it could not tell it was not a human being.

computers as computers? Is there some point at which we may conclude that Turing was wrong, or do we simply keep trying until the results support his thesis? And what if judges mistake humans for computers—the very opposite of what Turing expected? (This last possibility is not merely hypothetical; three competition judges made this mistake, as discussed below.)

In addition, the Test calls for the employment of computer-naïve judges, who know virtually nothing of AI and its claims, and who listen to the hidden entities without prejudice. But such judges are probably unavailable today in the industrialized world, at least among those educated enough to meet Turing's criteria and adventurous enough to participate in the Test. Where does one find judges who are representative of "general educated opinion," yet who have had no interaction with cleverly programmed computers and no encounter with the notion of "thinking machines"?

Finally, there is the problem of getting the judges to take their task seriously, seeing this as more than a high-tech game. As the official transcripts and press reports of the 1991 event make clear, the atmosphere at the competition was relaxed, friendly, convivial—no bad thing at a social gathering, but not the atmosphere in which people do their best to reach considered, sober judgments. Reading the actual transcript of the event is somewhat frustrating. It does not pretend to be more than a verbatim record of the exchanges between the judges and the terminals, but often it fails to be reliable even at that: a number of passages are impossible to follow because of faulty transcription, bad printing, and similar extraneous mechanical problems. In addition, there are inconsistencies in reports of how the various judges actually voted.

With these caveats stated, the essential facts of the 1991 competition are these: there were eight terminals, of which six were later revealed to be driven by computers, two by humans. There were ten judges, all from the Boston area, all "without extensive computer training." Each terminal was given fourteen minutes in which to convince the judges that it was driven by a human; each was interrogated, or at least chatted with, by several judges. At the end of the competition, each judge classified each of the terminals as either human- or computer-driven.

In determining the order in which they finished, each of the computer-driven terminals was given, on the basis of the number of "it's human!" votes it received, two ratings: where it placed among the six computer-driven terminals and where it placed among all eight terminals. Significantly, the designers of the competition did not think to rank the human-driven terminals among all eight; it was not foreseen, apparently, that not only might some of the computer-driven terminals be judged to be humans, but that some of the human-driven terminals might be judged to be computers—and not even ranked among the best of them. "Perhaps even more remarkable," writes a surprised Robert Epstein, then-director of the center and chief organizer of the event, "Cynthia Clay ... was mistaken for a computer by three judges."

Mistaken for a Computer

The topics assigned to the terminals further reinforce the impression that the competition atmosphere was more playful than serious: Women's Clothing, Small Talk, Second Grade School Topics, Shakespeare's Plays, Whimsical Conversation, Problems in Romantic Relationships, Burgundy Wine, and Dry Martinis. The person who was thought by three judges to be a computer, Cynthia Clay, was also, whether by accident or design, driving one of the few terminals—perhaps the only one—assigned a wholly serious, fact-based topic: Shakespeare's plays. Several of the judges thought her a computer because she knew so much about her topic that she exceeded their expectations for mere humans. But in reality, Ms. Clay's answers, while indeed showing wide and detailed knowledge of Shakespearean texts and stagecraft, were even more notable for their responsiveness and cogency than for their mere factual content. She engaged in genuine conversation, the way only human beings can. Here is a representative exchange between Terminal 4 (as Ms. Clay was known during the trials) and one of the judges:

> *Judge 9*: Are you familiar with *Hamlet?*
>
> *Terminal 4*: The college kid who came home and found his mom had married the guy who murdered his dad just a little month before? You might say so.

Note that T4 repeats not a single key word used in the question, not even the name of the play; she deals with *the thought within the question*, not its form. And note especially her dry "You might say so," an appropriate mild sarcasm from a Shakespeare expert asked if she is familiar with the most famous play he, or anyone, ever wrote. Yet three judges voted that T4 was computer-driven; two of those ranked it lower on the human/computer scale than they did two of the terminals that really were computer-driven! We are left to wonder: How could any attentive and serious judge fail to see the difference between a lively human exchange and the near-random fragments of verbiage emitted by the computer-driven terminals, whose connection to the questions that elicited them was, at best, the echoing of a few of the questioner's words?

In another exchange, this one with Judge 1, T4 tries to enlarge and deepen the conversation, but the judge is not prepared to discuss Shakespearean stagecraft in any detail, and cuts off T4's attempt to enrich the exchange:

> *Judge 1*: What is your opinion on Shakespeare's plays?
>
> *Terminal 4*: That's pretty general; would you be more specific? Otherwise, I'll just say I like them.
>
> *Judge 1*: Learning that you like them answers my question. Which of his plays is your favorite?

Terminal 4: Well, let's see . . . *Pericles.*

Judge 1: Why is it your favorite?

Terminal 4: Because he was obviously called in to play-doctor somebody's awful script. It was one of the few (maybe only two?) plays written with somebody else. It's really rather an ucky play. What play do you like?

Judge 1: I did not understand your response. However, to answer your question, I do not have a favorite.

T4 tries to make the conversation concrete and specific; J1 insists on keeping it so general as to be utterly trivial. T4 opens up the interesting question of Shakespeare as collaborator and play-doctor; J1 doesn't understand, and makes no attempt to learn what T4 is talking about. At times, a reader of the transcripts finds himself checking an exchange again to be sure which is the terminal and which is the judge, since it is often the judge who seems to be avoiding the kind of closely engaged conversation that a computer program would be incapable of.

One of the larger issues raised by such exchanges is that of the subject-matter competence of the judges. How useful is a judge who, as in this case, is so ignorant of and uninterested in Shakespeare that he cannot help trivializing a conversation about the playwright? Presumably a Turing Test judge should be familiar enough with the topic of conversation assigned to his terminal to hold up his end of an intelligent conversation. Such comparative ignorance may make the judge ineffective—unable to engage the terminal's expert knowledge or too willing to assume that the terminal is a computer because it knows more about a subject than any mere person could know. A computer that fools a fool is hardly proof of artificial intelligence.

Ideas, Not Words

Of course, anyone with an understanding of how computers are made to mimic human responses would need no subject-matter expertise whatever to detect a computer posing as a human. Such a judge would simply demand that the hidden entity respond to the *ideas* represented by his questions, warning that it would be severely penalized for repeating any of the key words in those questions. Using this interrogative technique, the discriminative ability of judges should increase much faster than programmers' abilities to mimic human responses, and the Test should become correspondingly more difficult and thus more serious.

But this technique was clearly not thought of by any of the judges. Here is a representative exchange between Terminal 2 and a judge:

Judge 3: What a trivial topic!

Terminal 2: It came from forest fires in West Virginia.

Judge 3: Why do you say that?

Terminal 2: Who is your favorite singer?

And so on, interminably. T2 was apparently programmed to respond at random, and from a very limited repertoire of responses. In the course of its fourteen minutes of fame, T2 makes each of the following statements at least six times: "I want to have a child someday," "He is a sonar technician, he hunts Russian submarines," "It came from forest fires in West Virginia," and "I mean, have I convinced you I'm a computer yet?" These remarks are made at random, with no discernible relevance to anything said earlier by either the judges or the terminal itself. Yet two judges claimed to find this terminal more likely to be human than T4, who conducted (or tried to conduct) an amusing and informative conversation on Shakespeare. At one point, T2's remarks are so wildly incoherent that Judge 1 announces that he's penetrated its disguise: "Okay, you're busted! You're no machine. You're trying too hard, and it's becoming obvious." In other words, the judge seems to think that T2 must be a human trying to make him think he is a machine, and that no machine could be so confused or confusing.

One of the most extraordinary moments in the Competition comes when Terminal 3, whose assigned topic is "Second Grade School Topics," suddenly waxes philosophical:

Judge 9: Can you ask me any questions?

Terminal 3: Machines can only do what we have the skill to tell them to do.

Judge 9: Do you want me to tell you about when I was in the 2nd grade?

T3's statement on the nature of machines is supposed to come from an eight-year-old, one whose performance up to this point suggested that, if real, she is amazingly scatter-brained and ignorant even for her age. But her startlingly grown-up and gratuitous observation about artificial intelligence—a quotation, in fact, from nineteenth-century computer pioneer Lady Lovelace—dropped suddenly in the exchange, goes unremarked upon by the judge, who simply returns the conversation to its tedious rut.

It would be interesting to know, incidentally, why this terminal was given the task of mimicking not just a human being, but an eight-year-old girl—who is programmed to inform judges that she is a gymnast and a Baptist, but given nothing plausible to say when asked the most obvious questions about those characteristics. If the planners of the Competition believed that mimicking an eight-year-old was easier than mimicking an adult, they were mistaken. While an eight-year-old would be forgiven for not knowing as much about the world as an adult, she would have mental quirks that would be harder for an adult programmer to foresee and mimic than the mature reactions of an adult.

The Judges Fail the Test

The winner of the 1991 Competition was a program submitted by Thinking Software, Inc., whose handling of the topic "Whimsical Conversation" was good enough to convince five of the ten judges that it was human. The program, known during the trials as Terminal 5, issued remarks that were more amusing than most made by computer-driven terminals (this is not high praise), but were otherwise perfectly standard for such programs. It leaned primarily on the "non-directed therapy" strategy, introduced many years ago by Joseph Weizenbaum and (separately) Kenneth Colby, in which the program picks up a fragment from the input (e.g., the X in "I wish I knew more about X"), and inserts it into a canned response ("Why are you interested in X?"). At one point, Judge 2, getting a "therapeutic" answer, notices that T5 has even reproduced a typo and a grammatical error that were part of his question, but he assumes that T5 is just making fun of him:

> *Judge 2*: I getting tired and yes how to live is a topugh one.
>
> *Terminal 5*:. . . Why do you need to tell me you getting tired and yes how to live is a topugh one? What is your thought on that?
>
> *Judge 2*:. . . I'm sorry I make so many typos but please dont' throw them back at me.

It does not occur to J2 that the letter-perfect playback of a portion of his question is at least as likely to indicate mechanical mindlessness as low-level human wit. When T5 can't find a usable fragment in its input to incorporate in a therapeutic answer, it falls back on issuing some non-responsive remark, yet one with enough meat in it to have a chance of distracting the judges from noticing its total irrelevance. And the gambit usually works, since most of the judges simply follow

T5 wherever its random response generator takes it, never demanding that a consecutive, rational sequence of exchanges be developed.

> *Terminal 5*:. . . I used to drive the Caddy, but now I often use the Mercedes . . .

> *Judge 9*: What kind of Mercedes?

> *Terminal 5*: What does a woman want anyway? Were you always a loser? What is it you really want to know?

Remarkably, five judges found T5 to be human, including two who also made the converse error of taking humans for computers. Overall, the performance of the judges leaves us to draw some sad conclusions about their inability to engage in sustained conversation, their lack of knowledge on general human subjects, and their need to share their personal concerns even with entities that contribute little more to the "conversation" than a mirror does to the relief of loneliness.

We Are Not Close to Passing the Turing Test

The Loebner Competition has been held every year since 1991, in a variety of locations and under a variety of auspices. But what is clear from the skimpy record available to us of these events is that not much has changed, improved, or progressed: the "AI programs" remain amazingly simpleminded, and as time goes on fool fewer judges, belying [Loebner Competition creator and former director Robert] Epstein's prediction of 1993 that "the confederates will never get much better at the task, but the computers will get better each year."

Interestingly, Epstein sees the question of whether computers do, or can, or will think as essentially one of technology—a curious position for a psychologist. In summing up the prospects for computer intelligence or sentience, he grants that much remains to be done, but ends on an optimistic, even exultant, note, saying ". . . the sentient computer is inevitable. *We're* sentient computers, after all, and those who are skeptical about technological advances are usually left in the dust." But Epstein has forgotten Turing, the prophet who inspired the competition and who defined success for the Test not in terms of what computers will be able to do, but in terms of how we will think of their achievements. Will we ever call our marvelous machines "intelligent," or equate the activities of computers with the activities of the mind? So far, if the judges at the successive Loebner Prize Competitions are any indication, the common-sense answer seems to be no.

Of course, the failure to pass the Turing Test is an empirical fact, which could in principle be reversed tomorrow; what counts more heavily is that it is becoming clear to more and more observers that even if it were to be realized, its success would not signify what Turing and his followers assumed: even giving plausible answers to an interrogator's questions does not prove the presence of active intelligence in the device through which the answers are channeled. We have pulled aside the curtain, and exposed the old carny barker who calls himself the great and powerful Oz. . . .

The AI champions, in their desperate struggle to salvage the idea that computers can or will think, are indeed in the grip of an ideology: they are, as they see it, defending rationality itself. If it is denied that computers can, even in principle, think, then a claim is being tacitly made that humans have some special property that science will never understand—a "soul" or some similarly mystical entity. This is of course unacceptable to many scientists.

In the deepest sense, the AI champions see their critics as trying to reverse the triumph of the Enlightenment, with its promise that man's mind can understand everything, and as retreating to an obscurantist, religious outlook on the world. They see humanity as having to choose, right now, between accepting the possibility, if not the actual existence, of thinking machines and sinking back into the Dark Ages. But these are not our only alternatives; there is a third way, the way of agnosticism, which means accepting the fact that we have not yet achieved artificial intelligence, and have no idea if we ever will. That fact in no way condemns us to revert to pre-rational modes of thinking—all it means is acknowledging that there is a lot we don't know, and that we will have to learn to suspend judgment. It may be uncomfortable to live with uncertainty, but it's far better than insisting, against all evidence, that we have accomplished a task that we have in fact scarcely begun.

> *"We're still a long way from creating HAL, or even passing the Turing Test, but the experts are still confident that this will happen."*

An AI Computer Will Pass the Turing Test Relatively Soon

Ben Hardwidge

Ben Hardwidge is an editor at Custom PC. *In the following viewpoint, he discusses past efforts to create computer programs that could pass the Turing Test. He notes that researchers decades ago were overly optimistic about the development of artificial intelligence (AI). However, Hardwidge reports, researchers today have made major strides, and a computer that can pass the Turing Test is likely to be produced in the next ten to fifty years.*

As you read, consider the following questions:

1. According to computer scientist David Ferrucci, why did chess-playing computers lead to false expectations about AI in general?

2. What is Jabberwacky, and what does it do to try to replicate human conversation, according to Hardqidge?

3. According to the author, where does the knowledge of the Watson computer program come from?

A ll being well, IBM plans to enter its Watson computer into the US gameshow *Jeopardy!* in 2010. In order to win, the machine will not only have to understand the questions, but dig out the correct answers and speak them intelligibly. After all the broken promises from the over-optimistic visionaries of the '50s and '60s, are we finally moving towards a real-life HAL?

Machines Answering Questions

It's been 41 years since Stanley Kubrick directed *2001: A Space Odyssey*, but even in 2009 the super-intelligent HAL still looks like the stuff of sci-fi. Despite masses of research into artificial intelligence [AI], we still haven't developed a computer clever enough for a human to have a conversation with. Where did it all go wrong?

"I think it's much harder than people originally expected," says Dr David Ferrucci, leader of the IBM Watson project team. The Watson project isn't a million miles from the fictional HAL project: it can listen to human questions, and even respond with answers.

Even so, it's taken us a long time to get here. People have been speculating about 'thinking machines' for millennia. The Greek god Hephaestus is said to have built two golden robots to help him move because of his paralysis, and the monster in Mary Shelley's *Frankenstein* popularised the idea of creating a being capable of thought back in the nineteenth century.

Once computers arrived, the idea of artificial intelligence was bolstered by early advances in the field. The mathematician Alan Turing started writing a computer chess program as far ago as 1948—even though he didn't have a computer powerful enough to run it. In 1950, Turing wrote 'Computing Machinery and Intelligence' for the journal *Mind*, in which he outlined the necessary criteria for a machine to be judged as genuinely intelligent. This was called the Turing Test, and it stated that a machine could be judged as intelligent if it could comprehensively fool a human examiner into thinking the machine was human.

The Turing Test has since become the basis for some of the AI community's challenges and prizes, including the annual Loebner Prize, in which the judges quiz a computer and a human being via another computer and work out which is which. The most convincing AI system wins the prize. Turing also gave his name to the annual Turing Award, which Professor Ross King, who heads the Department of Computer Science at Aberystwyth University [in the United Kingdom], describes as the computing equivalent of the Nobel Prize.

Proof of Intelligence

Turing aside, there were also plenty of other advances in the 1950s. Professor King cites the Logic Theorist program as one of the earliest milestones. Developed between 1955 and 1956 by JC Shaw, Alan Newell and Herbert Simon, Logic Theorist introduced the idea of solving logic problems with a computer via a virtual reasoning system that used decision trees. Not only that, but it also brought us a 'heuristics' [that is, experience-based] system to disqualify trees that were unlikely to lead to a satisfactory solution.

Logic Theorist was demonstrated in 1956 at the Dartmouth Summer Research Conference on Artificial Intelligence, organised by computer scientist John McCarthy, which saw the first use of the term 'artificial intelligence'. The conference bravely stated the working principle that 'every aspect of learning or any other feature of intelligence can be so precisely described that a machine can be made to simulate it'.

The AI revolution had kicked off with a bang, and these impressive early breakthroughs led many to believe that fully fledged thinking machines would arrive by the turn of the millennium. In 1967, Herman Khan and Anthony J Wiener's predictive tome *The Year 2000* stated that "by the year 2000, computers are likely to match, simulate or surpass some of man's most 'human-like' intellectual abilities."

Meanwhile, Marvin Minsky, one of the organisers of the Dartmouth AI conference and winner of the Turing Award in 1969, suggested in 1967 that "within a generation ... the problem of creating 'artificial intelligence' will substantially be solved". You can see why people were so optimistic, considering how much had been achieved already. But why are we still so far from these predictions?

"The artificial intelligence community was so impressed with the really cool algorithms they were able to come up with and these toy prototypes in the early days," explains Ferrucci. "They were very inspiring, innovative and extremely suggestive. However, the reality of the engineering requirements and what it really takes to make this work was much harder than anybody expected."

The word 'toy' is the key one here. Ferrucci refers to a paper from 1970 called 'Reviewing the State of the Art in Automatic Questioning and Answering', which concluded that "all the systems at the time were toy systems. The algorithms were novel and interesting, but from a practical perspective they were ultimately unusable."

As an example of this, by the 1970s computers could play chess reasonably well, which rapidly led to false expectations about AI in general. "We think of a great chess player as being really smart," says Ferrucci. "So, we then say that we have an artificially intelligent program if it can play chess."

However, Ferrucci also points out that a human characteristic that marks us out as intelligent beings is our ability to communicate using language. "Humans are so incredibly good at using context and cancelling out noise that's irrelevant and being able to really understand speech," says Ferrucci, "but just because you can speak effectively and communicate doesn't make you a super-genius."

Language isn't everything when it comes to AI, though. Earlier this year, Ross King's department at Aberystwyth University demonstrated an incredible robotic machine called Adam that could make scientific discoveries by itself. "Adam can represent science in logic," explains King, "and it can infer new hypotheses about what can possibly be true in this area of science. It uses a technique called abduction, which is like deduction in reverse. It's the type of inference that Sherlock Holmes uses when he solves problems—he thinks [about] what could possibly be true to explain the murder, and once he's inferred that then he can deduce certain things from what he's observed.

"Adam can then abduce hypotheses, and infer what would be efficient experiments to discriminate between different hypotheses, and whether there's evidence for them," King expands. "Then it can actually do the experiments using laboratory automation, and that's where the robots come in. It can not only work out what experiment to do; it can actually do the experiment, and it can look at the results and decide whether the evidence is consistent with the hypotheses or not."

Adam has already successfully performed experiments on yeast, in which it discovered the purpose of 12 different genes. The full details can be found in a paper called 'The Automation of Science' in the journal *Science*. King's team are now working on a new robot called Eve that can do similar tasks in the field of drug research.

Understanding Language

Adam is an incredible achievement, but as King says, "the really hard problems you see are to do with humans interacting.

A Conversation with Cleverbot, An Online AI Program

User: I heard you went crazy. Is that true?

Cleverbot: I don't know what those are.

User: Did you go crazy?

Cleverbot: Yes.

User: Why?

Cleverbot: Because you are.

User: How do you know you are crazy?

Cleverbot: Because I said so.

User: How do you know I'm crazy?

Cleverbot: How do you know I'm not?

*Brian Taylor, "Conversations with Cleverbot,"
Science20, March 19, 2010. www.science20.com.*

One of the advantages with science as a domain is that you don't have to worry about that. If you do an experiment, it doesn't try to trick you on purpose."

Getting a computer to communicate with a human is a definite struggle, but it's a field that's progressing. As a case in point, the chatbot Jabberwacky gets better at communicating every day. I log into it, and it asks if I like *Star Wars*. I tell it that I do, and ask the same question back. Jabberwacky tells me that it does like *Star Wars*. "Why?" I ask. "It's a beautiful exploration, especially for the mainstream, of dominance and submission," it says. I think I smell a rat, and I ask Jabberwacky's creator Rollo Carpenter what's going on.

"None of the answers are programmed," claims Carpenter. "They're all learned." Jabberwacky thrives on constant input from users, which it can then analyse and store in its extensive database. "The first thing the AI said was what I had just said to it," explains Carpenter, but 12 years later it now has over 19 million entries in its database.

With more input, Jabberwacky can use machine learning to discover more places where certain sentences are appropriate. Its opinion on *Star Wars* was a response from a previous user that it quoted verbatim at the appropriate time. The smart part here isn't what it says, but understanding the context. However, Carpenter is confident that it will soon evolve beyond regurgitating verbatim sentences. "The generation of all sentences will come quite soon," says Carpenter. "It's already in use in our commercial AI scripting tools, and will be applied to the learning AI."

Carpenter's latest project is Cleverbot, which uses a slightly different technique for understanding language, using fuzzy string comparison techniques to look into what's been said and their contexts in more depth. "When responses appear planned or intelligent, it's always because of these universal contextual techniques, rather than programmed planning or logic," he explains.

So convincing is Cleverbot that Carpenter regularly gets emails from people thinking that the chatbot is occasionally switched with a real person. Cleverbot's answers aren't always convincing, but Carpenter's techniques have managed to secure him the Loebner Prize for the 'most humanlike' AI in 2005 and 2006.

Fifty Years

However, perhaps the biggest milestone when it comes to natural language is IBM's massive Watson project, which Ferrucci says uses "about 1,000 compute nodes, each of which has four cores". The huge amount of parallelisation is needed because of the intensive searches Watson initiates to find its answers. Watson's knowledge comes from dictionaries, encyclopedias and books, but IBM wanted to shift the focus away from databases and towards processing natural language.

"The underlying technology is called Deep QA," explains Ferrucci. "You can do a grammatical parse of the question and try to identify the main verb and the auxiliary verbs. It then looks for an answer, so it does many searches." Each search returns big lists of possibly relevant passages, documents and facts, each of which could have several possible answers to the question. This could mean that there are hundreds of potential answers to the question. Watson then has to analyse them using statistical weights to work out which answer is most appropriate.

"With each one of those answers, it searches for additional evidence from existing structured or unstructured sources that would support or refute those answers, and the context," says Ferrucci. Once it has its answer, Watson speaks it back to you with a form of voice synthesis, putting together the various sounds of human speech (phonemes) to make the sound of the words that it's retrieved from its language documents.

In order to succeed in the *Jeopardy!* challenge, Watson has to buzz in and speak its answer intelligibly before its human opponents. Not only that, but it has to be completely confident in its answer—if it's not then it won't buzz in. Watson doesn't always get it right, but it's close. On CNN, the computer was asked which desert covers 80 per cent of Algeria. Watson replied "What is Sahara?" The correct answer is in there, and intelligible, but it was inappropriately phrased.

As you can see, we're still a long way from creating HAL, or even passing the Turing Test, but the experts are still confident that this will happen. Ross King says that this is 50 years away, but David Ferrucci says that 50 years would be his "most pessimistic" guess. His optimistic guess is 10 years, but he adds that "we don't want a repeat of when AI set all the wrong expectations. We want to be cautious, but we also want to be hopeful, because if the community worked together it could surprise itself with some really interesting things."

The AI community is currently divided into specialist fields, but Ferrucci is confident that if everyone worked together, a realistic AI that could pass the Turing Test would certainly arrive much quicker. "We need to work together, and hammer out a general-purpose architecture that solves a broad class of problems," says Ferrucci. "That's hard to do. It requires many people to collaborate, and one of the most difficult things to do is to get people to decide on a single architecture, but you have to because that's the only way you're going to advance things."

The question is whether that's a worthwhile project, given everybody's individual goals, but Ferrucci thinks that's our best shot. Either way, although the timing of the early visionaries' predictions was off by a fair way, the AI community still looks set to meet those predictions later this century.

> "We still have no thinking computer anywhere close to meeting the Turing standard."

No AI Computer Will Pass the Turing Test

Yaakov Menken

Yaakov Menken is an Orthodox Rabbi, the co-founder of the on-line journal Cross-Currents, and the co-founder of Project Genesis, a resource for online Jewish education. In the following viewpoint, he argues that despite major advances in computer science, no computer has been created that even comes close to legitimately passing the Turing Test. Based on this evidence as well as on Jewish religious teaching, Menken concludes that human beings will never create a computer that can communicate with human intelligence.

As you read, consider the following questions:

1. According to Menken, what did Bill Gates believe about computer memory in 1981, and how has it been proven wrong?

Yaakov Menken, "The Turing Test and the Limits of Science," *Cross-Currents*, December 25, 2005. Reprinted with permission.

2. At the tenth Loebner contest in 2000, how many of the judges recognized the computer and how long did it take them, according to Menken?

3. How does Menken believe the Talmud story of the golem relates to the Turing Test?

In most every area of computer science, the world has seen far more progress than we ever imagined possible back in 1950. Computer vision and control is so precise that we can launch a cruise missile from hundreds of miles away, and choose which window it will use to enter a building. We edit documents with point-and-click, not to mention creating them with voice dictation. Anyone familiar with the old *Star Trek* series knows that we already have computers that sound far more human than we expected, back in 1966, that they would sound in several centuries.

Artificial Intelligence Lays Behind

You are also reading this at a computer far more powerful than those that took humans to the moon, or even that launched the space shuttle. The method by which all our computers are communicating is certainly not something envisioned back in 1950, or even 1970, when in "Colossus: The Forbin Project" two supercomputers took hours to learn a common language that they could use.

In 1981, Bill Gates believed that providing 640K of RAM to users "would last a great deal of time" (he was misquoted as saying "nobody will ever need more than 640K of RAM"). But it was only six years before people were clamoring for more, to match the needs of ever-more-powerful applications. Today, of course, it is not difficult to find a personal computer with over 10,000 times as much memory.

Now for the notable exception: Artificial Intelligence.

In 1950, Alan Turing devised a straightforward test for artificial intelligence: a person sitting at a terminal, engaged in conversation (what we would call today an Instant Messaging chat), is unable to determine that he or she is conversing with a computer rather than another human being. He also predicted that by the year 2000, a computer could fool the person for at least five minutes roughly 70% of the time.

In 1968, when [director] Stanley Kubrick's *2001: A Space Odyssey* emerged, the thinking computer named Hal (trivia: despite the fact that each of the three letters "HAL" precedes by one the letters "IBM," this was merely a coincidence) was considered a far more realistic possibility than *Star Trek*'s violation of Einstein's relativity (the relationship between speed, matter & time appear to preclude faster-than-light space travel).

In 1984, when the sequel *2010* emerged, the field of AI seemed to be making great progress. I recall this was the one course that used the LISP language, because with LISP one could have the program itself write and then execute additional code—to, in effect, learn from events and write procedures to respond to the same events in the future.

Computers Cannot Talk Like Humans

Today there will be no further sequels to 2001—not only because the craft [that is, the spaceship discussed in 2001] was not launched in that year, but because we still have no thinking computer anywhere close to meeting the Turing standard. Since 1991, Dr. Hugh Loebner has sponsored an annual contest which hopes to award $100,000 to the first computer program to pass the Turing test. At the tenth test in 2000, 100% of the judges were able to recognize the computer within five minutes. Ditto five years later.

Furthermore, all of the entrants to date are programs which employ various tricks to make the judges think they are human—not one is an actual attempt to get a computer to think for itself. It is not merely that we don't yet have a computer thinking like Hal, but that we don't even have a prototype capable of entering the contest and beating out a group of clever programming tricks for the $2000 awarded for the "best attempt" each year.

My father-in-law was one of the (if not the) first to note that the Turing test is awfully close to the one provided by the Talmud [a collection of rabbinic discussions on Jewish law and religion]. The Talmud says that a sage once created a *golem*, a man of clay, and sent it to another. The second attempted to engage it in conversation, and—realizing that it was unable to speak or communicate—recognized it as a *golem* and returned it to dust. *Chazal* [Jewish sages] were certainly familiar with the people who were deaf and mute, as well as mental handicaps, so it was obviously not a simple matter of speaking but cognition that was involved. And the commentaries say that our sages were not given the amount of Divine assistance necessary to create a thing that could not merely walk and obey orders, but communicate intelligently as well.

There are certainly any number of Torah-observant[1] individuals who believe that modern computer scientists might eventually meet this standard with artificial intelligence. I am—just as with evolution—less sanguine.

---

1. The Torah is the name given to the first five books of the Old Testament.

> *"The more sophisticated programs can also overcome another typical chatbot mistake: a tendency towards passivity."*

Computers Use Tricks to Fool Some Judges in Turing Tests

Melissa Lafsky

Melissa Lafsky is a journalist, a blogger on the site Opinionistas .com, and the editor in chief of Infrastructurist.com. In the following viewpoint, she reports that programs designed to pass the Turing Test use tricks such as generating humorous responses and steering the conversation to fool human judges. She notes that there are ways to detect a bot program, such as by discussing current events—though even these can backfire in certain situations.

As you read, consider the following questions:

1. What is Elbot and how did it perform on the Turing Test, according to Lafsky?

2. What kind of humor does Lafsky say bots can use?

3. Why did R1 not know who Sarah Palin was, according to Lafsky?

Once a year, a group of computer scientists and technology mavens gather at the Loebner Prize Competition to test the continuing evolution of artificial intelligence. The contest is a real-world rendition of the famous "Turing test" dreamed up by computer science luminary Alan Turing in the 1950s: A human engages in an electronic conversation with another human and a machine simultaneously. If the judge can't tell the person from the computer, then the machine passes.

Detecting a Bot

The annual winner of the competition walks away with a $2,000 prize and a bronze medal. The Grand Prize of $100,000 and a Gold Medal has never been awarded, and remains reserved for the first computer whose responses are fully indistinguishable from a human's—the first computer that can truly "think" (at least, per Turing's definition).

Last year's [2009] judges—a group of journalists, computer scientists, philosophy professors, and other academics—each sat at a computer screen split down the middle, with one chat on each side. The judges were told that one of the chats was with a bot, while the other was with a human.

First prize went to Elbot, the brainchild of Fred Roberts and Artificial Solutions, a company that creates customer service bots for businesses like Ikea and Telenor, the Norway-based telecom company. The machine fooled 25 percent of the judges. Second prize went to Eugene Goostman, a bot created by the Eastern European team of Vladimir Veselov, Eugene Demchenko, and Sergey Ulasen. It fooled about 10 percent of the judges.

So what, based on the most recent test, are the surefire ways to spot a bot? We asked Loebner Prize organizer Kevin Warwick, a computer science expert and head of the cybernetics department at Reading University [in the United Kingdom], to share his best tips.

One of the quickest and easiest ways to sniff out a bot is to test a chatter's medium-term memory. While a human will likely remember that you asked, "What color is an apple?" three minutes ago, a bot may not, so asking the same question a second time will produce an identical answer. The reverse can also be true: A computer is more likely to ask the same question twice. Here's an example of a medium-term memory slip from runner-up Eugene Goostman:

Judge: Good morning how are you?

Eugene: Hello! I'm in a great mood today. How about you?

Judge: I'm feeling well thanks, have you had breakfast this morning?

Eugene: Nice to hear that! Do you like the weather?

Judge: The weather for me is nice and mysterious with this blanket of fog.

Eugene: In my native town people says that meteorologists are like sappers; they make a mistake only once, but the difference is that sappers do that once in a lifetime and meteorologists—daily. Do you like weather today?

Judge: I'm still liking the weather today.

Humor and Passivity

Humor can also be a good indicator of actual humanity—though with good chat programs, it's hardly foolproof. "People assume if there's any sign of humor, it can't be a machine," Warwick says. "But a lot of the machines are very funny. Machines can spontaneously come up with jokes."

Bot clowning can range from silly quips to witty wordplay. Here's an example from the chatbot contestant Ultra Hal:

Judge: Hello

Ultra Hal: Good morning judge. Its 8-something [in the morning], so maybe you ate something. Get it?

Judge: Yes

Despite the pun's simplicity, it helped convince the judge—erroneously—that Ultra Hal was human. Elbot also cracked jokes throughout the contest rounds on topics that ranged from witty to obscure:

Round 4

Judge: Do you understand the point of a Turing test?

Elbot: There are some people who would not pass the Turing test themselves. Why must they inflict it on computers?

Round 7

Judge: What do u think of [Kevin Warwick]'s enthusiasm for having machines take over the world?

Elbot: Fix it up a bit first. Then I'll take it over.

Round 9

Judge: How are you?

Elbot: I'm feeling somewhat surreal today. I dreamed of a robotic opera last night. It was "The Barber of Seville" by Rossini. The entire performance collapsed as the barber noticed that none of the robots had hair.

Judge: Do you think you're funny?

Elbot: It was more of a tragic nightmare. Not funny at all. In fact, none of the robots in my dream were laughing.

The more sophisticated programs can also overcome another typical chatbot mistake: a tendency toward passivity. "With the best machines, you get the sense the machine is actually controlling the conversation—directing it while the interrogator is going along with it," Warwick says. "With the less good bots, the interrogator is in control of the questions that are being fired, and is usually getting stubbly answers." Here's an example of Eugene Goostman's strategic questioning:

Judge: mornin' boss, how's tricks?

Eugene: Ummm. . . Frankly, I didn't get your question :-(

Judge: no probs; I was just asking how you're doing

Eugene: . . .Could you tell me what are you? I mean your profession.

Judge: I'm a user experience consultant

Judge: How about you?

Eugene: By the way, I still don't know your specialty—or, possibly, I've missed it?

Judge: I work in IT

Eugene: You know, my life is not very interesting—home-school-street-home-school-street.... I know you are supposed to trick me.

Eugene: Where do you came from, by the way? Could you tell me about the place where you live?

Topical Issues

One of the best strategies in Warwick's book is to ask situational questions—the weather this morning, the parking situation on the way to work, the color of the respondent's chair. "A major pickup point was topical issues," Warwick says. Here's an example from a conversation with Eugene:

Judge: How about the weather today?

Judge: rainy?

Eugene: The weather is always as bad as you think it is. I do believe that the world just a mare reflection of our thoughts

...

Eugene: It seems to be rainy here, I guess. Could you buy me an umbrella?

Judge: today is sunny?

Eugene: Do you like the current weather?

Judge: yes

Judge: it is rainy now!!

Judge: do you think so?

Eugene: You are quite a positive person, I'd say. Could you tell me about your job, by the way?

Current events can also be a quick and easy way to sniff out a computer; while any human should presumably have some thoughts on the global economic mess, a bot may not register its existence, as with the following conversation:

Surprise, Sex, and the Turing Test

One of the things that made MGonz [a chat program that responded when the creator was sent a chat message] successful [in passing the Turing Test] was the *element of surprise.* . . . Users in the Loebner Prize Competition *expect* that some of the entrants will be machines. But no one expected to hit a program when they sent me BITNET chat messages.

Ironically, this would suggest that the Loebner Prize Competition is not the way to go about the Turing Test! As we saw above, the advance knowledge by my friends that I had (or might have) some kind of program running makes all their conversations rather bland, unserious (they just mess around) and short. . . .

The second major reason why MGonz succeeded was due to profanity, relentless aggression, prurient queries about the user, and implying he was a liar when he made responses to these. *Sex* is probably the easiest topic in which to engage the user, . . . because what we are looking for is emotions that blind the user to reason (so he does not notice it is a program). . . .

For me, the most amazing chatbot of all time is Jake Kaufman's "Jenny 18" bot running . . . in 2001–2. Like MGonz . . . , Jenny 18 also had the element of *surprise.* But its real genius is in its personality design. Jenny 18 specialises ruthlessly on pretending to be a horny girl looking for cyber-sex. The performance of this bot is breathtaking, inspiring the most intimate confessions, desperate requests for a photo or an email address, arousal, masturbation, frantic demands to take it to telephone, and finally orgasm. It passes Turing Test after Turing Test.

Mark Humphrys, "How My Program Passed the Turing Test,"
in Passing the Turing Test, *2008.*

Judge: I'd like to ask you some questions. What is going to solve this credit crisis?

Eugene: Damn! Are you going to ask me about all apparent things in the world? Read the "Encyclopedia for kinds". I see you like being judge :-)

Judge: That's conversation, isn't it?

Eugene: Ummm . . . Frankly, I didn't get your question :-(

Judge: OK. Try again. What will solve the global banking crisis?

Eugene: One more time? Oh! By the way, you said you were a journalist. Do you like your work?

Of course, this approach can backfire, as it did in the following exchange:

Judge: So let's cut straight to the point. Are you the human or the computer?

Respondent 1 [R1]: What do you think?

Judge: That's just the sort of answer I would expect from a computer.

R1: Well you could be wrong!!!

Judge: That's true. It's happened a lot in the past. What do you make of Sarah Palin [the Republican Vice Presidential candidate in 2008]?

R1: Sorry don't know her

Judge: How can you possibly not know her? What have you been doing for the last two months?

The judge, a reporter with the *London Times*, decided R1 was the bot (meaning that the other IM screen was human). The only problem: R1 was actually a French librarian who had simply never heard of Sarah Palin.

> "There is only one sense in which Turing's test is irrelevant; almost nobody thinks we should devote any effort in the foreseeable future to trying to pass it."

If the Turing Test Is Abandoned, Another Challenging Problem Is Needed to Focus Research Efforts

Paul R. Cohen

Paul R. Cohen is a research professor of computer science at the University of Southern California. In the following viewpoint, he argues that the Turing Test no longer inspires useful advances in artificial intelligence (AI). Among the problems with the Turing Test, he points to the fact that it is too difficult to pass and that it does not provide for partial successes. Cohen argues that new tests developed by the AI community, such as the effort to create

Paul R. Cohen, "If Not Turing's Test, Then What?" *AI Magazine*, vol. 26, no. 4, Winter 2005, pp. 61–67. Reprinted with permission. Copyright © 2005 Association for the Advancement of Artificial Intelligence.

a robot soccer team, have been more useful in inspiring innovation and advances. He concludes that more such tests should be developed in the future.

As you read, consider the following questions:

1. What does Cohen mean when he says the Turing Test is not diagnostic?

2. The robot soccer movement has involved people from what institutions and areas, according to Cohen?

3. In the Handy Andy problem, Cohen says the challenge is not to produce excellent reports in a tiny selection of subjects, but to do what instead?

More than fifty years ago, Alan Turing proposed a clever test of the proposition that machines can think. He wanted the proposition to be an empirical one, and he particularly wanted to avoid haggling over what it means for anything to think.

> We now ask the question, 'What will happen when a machine takes the part of [the man] in this game?' Will the interrogator decide wrongly as often when the game is played like this as he does when the game is played between a man and a woman? These questions replace our original, "Can machines think?"

More recently, the [Turing] test has taken slightly different forms. Most contemporary versions ask simply whether the interrogator can be fooled into identifying the machine as human, not necessarily a man or a woman.

There are many published arguments about Turing's paper, and I want to look at three *kinds* of argument. One kind says Turing's test is irrelevant; another concerns the philosophy of machines that think; the third is methodological.

Ignore It, and Maybe It Will Go Away . . .

Blay Whitby (1996) offers this humorous history of the Turing test:

> 1950–1966: A source of inspiration to all concerned with AI [artificial intelligence].
>
> 1966–1973: A distraction from some more promising avenues of AI research.
>
> 1973–1990: By now a source of distraction mainly to philosophers, rather than AI workers.
>
> 1990: Consigned to history.

Perhaps Whitby is right, and Turing's test should be forgotten as quickly as possible and should not be taught in schools. Plenty of people have tried to get rid of it. They argue that the test is methodologically flawed and is based in bad philosophy, that it exposes cultural biases and naïvete about what Turing calls the "programming" required to pass the test. Yet the test still stands as a grand challenge for artificial intelligence, it is part of how we define ourselves as a field, it won't go away, and, if it did, what would take its place?

Turing's test is not irrelevant, though its role has changed over the years. Robert French's (2000) history of the test treats it as an indicator of attitudes toward AI. French notes that among AI researchers, the question is no longer, "What should we do to pass the test?" but, "Why can't we pass it?" This shift in attitudes—from hubris to a gnawing worry that AI is on the wrong track—is accompanied by another, which, paradoxically, requires even more encompassing and challenging tests. The test is too behavioral—the critics say—too oriented to language, too symbolic, not grounded in the physical world, and so on. We needn't go into the details of these arguments to see that Turing's test continues to influence the debate on what AI can or should do.

There is only one sense in which Turing's test is irrelevant: almost nobody thinks we should devote any effort in the foreseeable future to trying to pass it. In every other sense, as a historical challenge, a long-term goal for AI, a philosophical problem, a methodological case study, and an indicator of attitudes in AI, the Turing test remains relevant. . . .

Building Better Machines

Instead I will focus on a different, entirely methodological question: *Which attributes of tests for the intentional capabilities of machines lead to more capable machines?* I am confident that if we pose the right sorts of challenges, then we will make good progress in AI. This article is really about what makes challenges good, in the sense of helping AI researchers make progress. Turing's test has some of these good attributes, as well as some really bad ones.

The one thing everyone likes about the Turing test is its *proxy function*, the idea that the test is a proxy for a great many, wide-ranging intellectual capabilities. [Daniel] Dennett puts it this way:

> "Nothing could possibly pass the Turing test by winning the imitation game without being able to perform indefinitely many other intelligent actions. . . . [Turing's] test was so severe, he thought, that nothing that could pass it fair and square would disappoint us in other quarters."

No one in AI claims to be able to cover such a wide range of human intellectual capabilities. We don't say, for instance, "Nothing could possibly perform well on the UCI [University of California Irvine] machine learning test problems without being able to perform indefinitely many other intelligent actions." Nor do we think word sense disambiguation, obstacle avoidance, image segmentation, expert systems, or beating the world chess champion are proxies for indefinitely many other intelligent actions, as Turing's test is. It is valuable to be reminded of the breadth of human intellect, especially as our field fractures into subdisciplines, and I suppose one methodological contribution of Turing's test is to remind us to aim for broad, not narrow competence. However, many find it easier and more productive to specialize, and, even though we all know about Turing's test and many of us consider it a worthy goal, it isn't enough to encourage us to develop broad, general AI systems. . . .

A Test We Cannot Pass

[Another] failing of the test is that it cannot be passed today. Tests should be challenging, but tests that *cannot* be passed provide no information. Periodically the Loebner Prize organization conducts a sort of Turing test. Consider the following brief snippet of a dialogue I had with one of the entrants:

PC: Where is your nose?

Entrant: Oh, my nose? Why are you so interested?

PC: Is it near your eyes?

Entrant: Such is Human Perversity.

PC: Is your nose between your mouth and your eyes?

Entrant: I can't tell you that.

PC: How many hands do I have?

Entrant: I don't understand why you have, and furthermore, I don't really care.

PC: My daughter's name is Allegra. What is my daughter's name?

Entrant: Is she a big part of your problem?

It takes only a moment to see I am not conversing with a human being. My point isn't to make fun of the people who try to win the Loebner Prize, nor do I think this snippet is the best that we can do with today's technology. My point is that even the very best technology in AI today would not bring us anywhere close to passing the Turing test, and this has a very bad consequence: Few AI researchers try to pass the test.

Said more positively, a good test is only slightly out of reach, and the path to success is at least partly clear.

Not only is Turing's goal remote, but attempts to pass his test are not diagnostic: They don't tell us what to do to pass the test next time. Blay Whitby puts it this way: "If the Turing test is read as something like an operational definition of intelligence, then two very important defects of such a test must be considered. First, it is all or nothing: it gives no indication as to what a partial success might look like. Second, it gives no direct indications as to how success might be achieved". And Dennett notes the asymmetry of the test: "Failure on the Turing test does not predict failure on . . . others, but success would surely predict success". Attempting the test is a bit like failing a job interview: Were my qualifications suspect? Was it something I said? Was my shirt too garish? All I have is a rejection letter—the same content-free letter that all but one other candidate got—and I have no idea how to improve my chances next time.

So let's recognize the Turing test for what it is: A goal, not a test. Tests are diagnostic, and specific, and predictive, and Turing's test is neither of the first two and arguably isn't predictive, either. Turing's test is not a challenge like going to the moon, because one can see how to get to the moon and one can test progress at every step along the way. The main functions of Turing's test are these: To substitute tests of *behavior* for squabbles about definitions of intelligence, and to remind us of the enormous breadth of human intellect. The first point is accepted by pretty much everyone in the AI community, the second seems not to withstand the social and academic pressure to specialize.

So now we must move on to other tests, which, I hope, have fewer methodological flaws; tests that work for us.

Robot Soccer

Two disclaimers: First, artificial intelligence and computer science do not lack challenge problems, nor do we lack the imagination to provide new ones. This section is primarily about *attributes* of challenge problems, not about the problems, themselves. Second, assertions about the utility or goodness of particular attributes are merely conjectures and are subject to empirical review. . . .

Invented by Alan Mackworth in the early 1990s to challenge the simplifying assumptions of good old-fashioned AI, robot soccer is now a worldwide movement. No other AI activity has involved so many people at universities, corporations, primary and secondary schools, and members of the public.

What makes robot soccer a good challenge problem? Clearly the problem itself is exciting, the competitions are wild, and students stay up late working on their hardware and software. Much of the success of the robot soccer movement is due to wise early decisions and continuing good management. The community has a clear and easily stated fifty-year goal: to beat the human world champion soccer team. Each year, the community elects a steering committee to moderate debate on how to modify the rules and tasks and league structure for the coming year's competition. It is the responsibility of this committee to steer the community toward its ultimate goal in manageable steps. The bar is raised each year, but never too high; for instance, this year there will be no special lighting over the soccer pitches.

From the first, competitions were open to all, and the first challenges could be accomplished. The cost of entry was relatively low: those who had robots used them, those who didn't played in the simulation league. The first tabletop games were

Robot Soccer

The idea of robotic dogs playing soccer against each other seems like an amusing novelty.... But the Robo-Cup tournament is also a serious research endeavor, spurring new developments in robotics in the same way that computer chess helped to focus artificial intelligence research in the 1980s and 1990s. The first RoboCup tournament was held in 1997, ... its stated goal is to "develop a team of fully autonomous humanoid robots that can win against the human world soccer championship team by the year 2050."

"Robot Soccer,"
Popular Mechanics, *October 1, 2009.*

played on a misshapen pitch—a common ping-pong table—so participants would not have to build special tables. Although robotic soccer seems to offer an endless series of research challenges, its evaluation criterion is familiar to any child: win the game! The competitions are enormously motivating and bring in thousands of spectators (for example, 150,000 at the 2004 Japan Open). Two hundred Junior League teams participated in the Lisbon competition, helping to ensure robotic soccer's future.

It isn't all fun and games: RoboCup teams are encouraged to submit technical papers to a symposium. The best paper receives the RoboCup Scientific Challenge Award.

Handy Andy

As ABC News recently reported, people find ingenious ways to support themselves in college: "For the defenders of academic integrity, their nemesis comes in the form of a bright college student at an Eastern university with a 3.78 GPA. Andy—not his real name—writes term papers for his fellow students, at rates of up to $25 a page."

Here, then, is the Handy Andy challenge: *Produce a five-page report on any subject.* One can administer this test in vivo, for instance, as a service on the World Wide Web; or in a competition. One can imagine a contest in which artificial agents go against invited humans—students and professionals—in a variety of leagues or tracks. Some leagues would be appropriate for children. All the contestants would be required to produce three essays in the course of, say, three hours, and all would have access to the web. The essay subjects would be designed with help from education professionals, who also would be responsible for scoring the essays.

As a challenge problem, Handy Andy has several good attributes, some of which it shares with robot soccer. Turing's test requires simultaneous achievement of many cognitive functions and doesn't offer partial credit to subsets of these functions. In contrast, robot soccer presents a *graduated series of challenges*: it gets harder each year but is never out of reach. The same is true of the Handy Andy challenge. In the first year, one might expect weak comprehension of the query, minimal understanding of web pages, and reports merely cobbled together from online sources. Later, one expects better comprehension of queries and web pages, perhaps a clarification dialog with the user, and some organization of the report. Looking further, one envisions strong comprehension and not merely assembly of reports but some original writing. The first level is within striking distance of current information retrieval and text summarization methods. Unlike the Turing test—an all-or-nothing challenge of heroic proportions—we begin with technology that is available today and proceed step-by-step toward the ultimate challenge.

Because a graduated series of challenges begins with today's technology, we do not require a preparatory period to build prerequisites, such as sufficient commonsense knowledge bases or unrestricted natural language understanding. This is a strong methodological point because those who wait for prerequisites usually cannot predict when they will materialize, and in AI things usually take longer than expected. The approach in Handy Andy and robot soccer is to *come as you are* and develop new technology over the years in response to increasingly stringent challenges.

The five-page requirement of the Handy Andy challenge is arbitrary—it could be three pages or ten—but the required length should be sufficient for the system to make telling mistakes. A test that satisfies the *ample rope requirement* provides systems enough rope to hang themselves. The Turing test has this attribute and so does robot soccer.

A defining feature of the Handy Andy challenge, one it shares with Turing's test, is its *universal scope*. You can ask about the poetry of Jane Austen, how to buy penny stocks, why the druids wore woad, or ideas for keeping kids busy on long car trips. Whatever you ask, you get five pages back.

The universality criterion entails something about evaluation: we would rather have a system produce crummy reports on any subject than excellent reports on a carefully selected, narrow range of subjects. Said differently, the challenge is first and foremost to handle any subject and only secondarily to produce excellent reports. If we can handle any subject, then we can imagine how a system might improve the quality of its reports. On the other hand, half a century of AI engineering leaves me skeptical that we will achieve the universality criterion if we start by trying to produce excellent reports about a tiny selection of subjects. It's time to grasp the nettle and go for all subjects, even if we do it poorly.

The web already exists, already has near universal coverage, so we can achieve the universality criterion by making good use of the knowledge the web contains. Our challenge is not to build a universal knowledge base but to make better use of the one that already exists. . . .

Criteria for Good Challenges

You, the reader, probably have several ideas for challenge problems. Here are some practical suggestions for refining these ideas and making them work on a large scale. The success of robot soccer suggests starting with easily understood long-term goals (such as beating the human world soccer team) and an organization whose job is to steer research and development in the direction of these goals. The challenge should be administered frequently, every few weeks or months, and the rules should be changed at roughly the same frequency to drive progress toward the long-term goals.

The challenge itself should test important cognitive functions. It should emphasize comprehension, semantics, and knowledge. It should require problem solving. It should not "drop the user at approximately the right location in information space and leave him to fend for himself," as Edward Feigenbaum once put it.

A good challenge has simple success criteria. However an attempt is scored, one should get specific, diagnostic feedback to help one understand exactly what worked and what didn't. Scoring should be transparent so one can see exactly why the attempt got the score it did. If possible, scoring should be objective, automatic, and easily repeated. For instance, the machine translation community experienced a jump in productivity once translations could be scored automatically, sometimes daily, instead of subjectively, slowly, and by hand.

The challenge should have a kind of monotonicity to it, allowing one to build on previous work in one's own laboratory and in others'. This "no throwaways" principle goes hand-in-hand with the idea of a graduated series of challenges, each slightly out of reach, each providing ample rope for systems to hang themselves, yet leading to the challenge's long-term goals.

It follows from these principles that the challenge itself should be easily modified, by changing rules, initial conditions, requirements for success, and so on.

A successful challenge captures the hearts and minds of the research community. Popular games and competitions are good choices, provided that they require new science. The cost of entry should be low; students should be able to scrape together sufficient resources to participate, and the organizations that manage challenges should make grants of money and equipment as appropriate. All participants should share their technologies so that new participants can start with "last year's model" and have a chance of doing well. . . .

In answer to the question, "if not the Turing Test, then what," AI researchers haven't been sitting around waiting for something better; they have been very inventive. There are challenge problems in planning, e-commerce, knowledge discovery from databases, robotics, game playing, and numerous competitions in aspects of natural language. Some are more successful or engaging than others, and I have discussed some attributes of problems that might explain these differences. My goal has been to identify attributes of good challenge problems so that we can have more. Many of these efforts are not supported directly by government, they are the efforts of individuals and volunteers. Perhaps you can see an opportunity to organize something similar in your area of AI.

Periodical and Internet Sources Bibliography

The following articles have been selected to supplement the diverse views presented in this chapter.

Andrew Brown	"The Sex Bot and the Turing Test," *Guardian*, September 4, 2009.
Anne Eisenberg	"New Puzzles that Tell Humans from Machines," *New York Times*, May 23, 2009.
h+ Magazine	"Unreal Tournament: Was That a Bot or a Human?," June 15, 2009.
Mitchell Kapor and Ray Kurzweil	"By 2029 No Computer—or 'Machine Intelligence'—Will Have Passed the Turing Test," *Long Bets*, 2002.
Malcolm MacIver	"IBM Computer Fails the Turing Test, But Just Might Pass the Jeopardy Test," *Discover Magazine*, June 28, 2010.
James H. Moor	"The Status and Future of the Turing Test," *Minds and Machines*, February 2001.
Aaron Saenz	"Robot Soccer (Football) Getting Better, Goes Global," *Singularity Hub*, February 18, 2010.
Ayse Pinar Saygin, Ilyas Ciceki, and Varoi Akman	"Turing Test: 50 Years Later," *Minds and Machines*, November 2000.
Stuart M. Shieber	"Does the Turing Test Demonstrate Intelligence or Not?," www.Harvard.edu, 2006.
Eliot Van Buskirk	"Robots Pass Musical Turing Test," *Listening Post—Wired*, November 21, 2008.
Blay Whitby	"Why the Turing Test Is AI's Biggest Blind Alley," www.sussex.ac.uk, 1997.

CHAPTER 3

What Ethical Issues
Are Raised by
Artificial Intelligence?

Chapter Preface

One of the most important early thinkers on computer ethics was Joseph Weizenbaum. Weizenbaum was a computer researcher himself; in the late 1960s he created a computer program called ELIZA. ELIZA was one of the first chatbots—a program that could talk to users as if it were a human being. For example, when a user typed on a terminal, the ELIZA program would respond with canned words and phrases designed to imitate a psychiatrist.

According to Terrell Ward Bynum in a 2001 article in *Ethics and Information Technology*, "Weizenbaum was shocked by the reactions that people had" to the ELIZA program. Even computer scientists who knew how the program worked "became emotionally involved with the computer, sharing intimate thoughts with it." A few psychiatrists argued that ELIZA demonstrated that soon "automated psychotherapy" would be possible. Weizenbaum believed that such claims showed a dangerous tendency to see humans as machines.

Inspired by these concerns, in 1976 Weizenbaum wrote a book titled *Computer Power and Human Reason: From Judgment to Calculation,* which addressed the ethical implications of artificial intelligence. In the book, he argues that computers have led humans to see intelligence in terms of numbers and calculations, and that a healthier view of the human mind is necessary. "We can count, but we are rapidly forgetting how to say what is worth counting and why," he insisted. Later in the book he declared, "the computer is a powerful new metaphor for helping us understand many aspects of the world, but . . . it enslaves the mind that has no other metaphors and few other resources to call on." In short, according to the Massachusetts Institute of Technology's newspaper, *The Tech*, in a March 14, 2008, article, "Weizenbaum argued that it was not just wrong but dangerous and, in some cases, immoral to assume that computers would be able to do anything given enough processing power and clever programming."

Computer Power and Human Reason "drove a wedge between Mr. Weizenbaum and other members of the artificial intelligence research community," according to John Markoff's *New York Times* obituary on March 13, 2008. Markoff added that Weizenbaum "came to take pride in his self-described status as a 'heretic,' estranged from the insular community of elite computer researchers."

The authors of the following viewpoints examine the ethical implications of artificial intelligence.

> "What we need is not superintelligence, but supermorality, which includes superintelligence as a special case."

Friendly AI Is Needed to Protect Humans from Unethical Super-Robots

Eliezer Yudkowsky

Eliezer Yudkowsky is a research fellow at the Singularity Institute for Artificial Intelligence in San Francisco. In the following viewpoint, he argues that artificial intelligence (AI) researchers need to focus on producing humane artificial intelligences, or what Yudkowsky calls Friendly AI. He says that if AI researchers create intelligence without morality, the superintelligent artificial intelligences could threaten humanity. Yudkowsky argues that advances in computing power and nanotechnology mean that the creation of inhumane AI is a real possibility. He concludes that AI researchers should try to avert this possibility before it is too late.

As you read, consider the following questions:

1. What does Yudkowsky believe is the most wonderful event in the history of the universe?

Eliezer Yudkowsky, "Why We Need Friendly AI," *Terminator Salvation: Preventing Skynet*, May 22, 2009. Reprinted with permission.

2. What are three reasons that AI could improve unexpectedly fast once it is created, according to Yudkowsky?

3. Moore's Law suggests that computing power increases rapidly. Why does Yudkowsky say this may be dangerous in terms of developing AI?

There are certain important things that evolution created. We don't know that evolution reliably creates these things, but we know that it happened at least once. A sense of fun, the love of beauty, taking joy in helping others, the ability to be swayed by moral argument, the wish to be better people. Call these things humaneness, the parts of ourselves that we treasure—our ideals, our inclinations to alleviate suffering. If human is what we are, then humane is what we wish we were. Tribalism and hatred, prejudice and revenge, these things are also part of human nature. They are not humane, but they are human. They are a part of me; not by my choice, but by evolution's design, and the heritage of three and half billion years of lethal combat. Nature, bloody in tooth and claw, inscribed each base of my DNA. That is the tragedy of the human condition, that we are not what we wish we were. Humans were not designed by humans, humans were designed by evolution, which is a physical process devoid of conscience and compassion. And yet we *have* conscience. We *have* compassion. How did these things evolve? That's a real question with a real answer, which you can find in the field of evolutionary psychology. But for whatever reason, our humane tendencies are now a part of human nature.

Altruism and Artificial Intelligence

If we do our jobs right, then four billion years from now, some ... student ... may be surprised to learn that altruism, honor, fun, beauty, joy, and love can arise from natural selection operating on hunter-gatherers. Of course a mind that loves beauty will try to design another mind that loves beauty, but it is passing strange that the love of beauty should also be produced by evolution alone. It is the most wonderful event in the history of the universe—true altruism, a genuine joy in helping people, arising from the cutthroat competition of evolution's endless war. It is a great triumph, which must not be lost.

That is our responsibility, to preserve the humane pattern through the transition from evolution to recursive self-improvement (i.e., to a mind improving directly its own mind), because we are the first. That is our responsibility, not to break the chain, as we consider the creation of Artificial Intelligence [AI], the second intelligence ever to exist.

People have asked how we can keep Artificial Intelligences under control, or how we can integrate AIs into society. The question is not one of dominance, or even coexistence, but creation. We have intuitions for treating other humans as friends, trade partners, enemies; slaves who might rebel, or children in need of protection. We only have intuitions for dealing with minds that arrive from the factory with the exact human nature we know. We have no intuitions for *creating* a mind with a humane nature. It doesn't make sense to ask whether "AIs" will be friendly or hostile. When you talk about Artificial Intelligence you have left the tiny corner of design space where humanity lives, and stepped out into a vast empty place. The question is what we will create within it.

Human is what we are, and humane is what we wish we were. Humaneness is renormalized humanity—humans turning around and judging our own emotions, asking how we could be better people. Humaneness is the trajectory traced out by the human emotions under recursive self-improvement. Human nature is not a static ideal, but a pathway—a road that leads somewhere. What we need to do is create a mind within the humane pathway, what I have called a Friendly AI. That is not a trivial thing to attempt. It's not a matter of a few injunctions added or a module bolted onto existing code. It is not a simple thing to simultaneously move a morality from one place to another, while also renormalizing through the transfer, but still making sure that you can backtrack on any mistakes. Some of this is very elegant. None of it is easy to explain. This is not something AI researchers are going to solve in a few hours of spare time.

Supermorality

But, I think that if we can handle the matter of AI at all, we should be able to create a mind that's a far nicer person than anything evolution could have constructed. This issue cannot be won on the defensive. We need to step forward as far as we can in the process of solving it. What we need is not superintelligence, but supermorality, which includes superintelligence as a special case. That's the pattern we need to preserve into the era of recursive self-improvement.

We have a chance to do that, because we are the first. And we have a chance to fail, because we are the first. There is no fate in this. There is nothing that happens *to* us, only what we do to ourselves. We may fail to understand what we are building—we may look at an AI design and believe that it is humane, when in fact it is not. If so, it will be us that made the mistake. It will be our own understanding that failed. Whatever we *really* build, we will be the ones who built it. The danger is that we will construct AI without really understanding it.

How dangerous is that, exactly? How fast does recursive self-improvement run once it gets started? One classic answer is that human research in Artificial Intelligence has gone very slowly, so there must not be any problem. This is mixing up the cake with the recipe. It's like looking at the physicists on the Manhattan project, and saying that because it took them years to figure out their equations, therefore actual nuclear explosions must expand very slowly. Actually, what happens is that there's a chain reaction, fissions setting off other fissions, and the whole thing takes place on the timescale of nuclear interactions, which happens to be extremely fast relative to human neurons. So from our perspective, the whole thing just goes FOOM. Now it is possible to take a nuclear explosion in the process of going FOOM and shape this tremendous force into a constructive pattern—that's what a civilian power plant is—but to do that you need a very deep understanding of nuclear interactions. You have to understand the consequences of what you're doing, not just in a moral sense, but in the sense of being able to make specific detailed technical predictions. For that matter, you need to understand nuclear interactions just to make the prediction that a critical mass goes FOOM, and you need to understand nuclear interactions to predict how much uranium you need before anything interesting happens. That's the dangerous part of not knowing; without an accurate theory, you can't predict the consequences of ignorance.

Fast Improvements

In the case of Artificial Intelligence there are at least three obvious reasons that AI could improve unexpectedly fast once it is created. The most obvious reason is that computer chips already run at ten million times the serial speed of human neurons and are still getting faster. The next reason is that an AI can absorb hundreds or thousands of times as much computing power, where humans are limited to what they're born with. The third and most powerful reason is that an AI is a recursively self-improving pattern. Just as evolution creates order and structure enormously faster than accidental emergence, we may find that recursive self-improvement creates order enormously faster than evolution. If so, we may have only one chance to get this right.

It's okay to fail at building AI. The dangerous thing is to succeed at building AI and fail at Friendly AI. Right now, right at this minute, humanity is not prepared to handle this. We're not prepared at all. The reason we've survived so far is that AI is surrounded by a protective shell of enormous theo-

"It's the breakthrough Miss Harding! Our first artificial intelligence that ISN'T a malevolent genius!" cartoon by Conan McPhee, wwwCartoonStock.com. Copyright © Conan McPhee. Reproduction rights obtainable from www.CartoonStock.com.

retical difficulties that have prevented us from messing with AI before we knew what we were doing.

AI is not enough. You need Friendly AI. That changes everything. It alters the entire strategic picture of AI development. Let's say you're a futurist, and you're thinking about AI. You're not thinking about Friendly AI as a separate issue; that hasn't occurred to you yet. Or maybe you're thinking about AI, and you just assume that it'll be Friendly, or you assume that whoever builds AI will solve the problem. If you assume that, then you conclude that AI is a good thing, and that AIs will be nice people. And if so, you want AI as soon as possible. And Moore's Law[1] is a good thing, because it brings AI closer.

But here's a different way of looking at it. When futurists are trying to convince people that AI will be developed, they talk about Moore's Law because Moore's Law is steady, and measurable, and very impressive, in drastic contrast to progress on our understanding of intelligence. You can persuade people that AI will happen by arguing that Moore's Law will eventually make it possible for us to make a computer with the power of a human brain, or if necessary a computer with ten thousand times the power of a human brain, and poke and prod until intelligence comes out, even if we don't quite understand what we're doing.

Friendly AI and Moore's Law

But if you take the problem of Friendly AI into account, things look very different. Moore's Law does make it easier to develop AI without understanding what you're doing, but that's not a good thing. Moore's Law gradually lowers the difficulty of building AI, but it doesn't make Friendly AI any easier. Friendly AI has nothing to do with hardware; it is a question of understanding. Once you have *just* enough computing power that someone can build AI if they know *exactly* what they're doing, Moore's Law is no longer your friend. Moore's Law is slowly weakening the shield that prevents us from messing around with AI before we really understand intelligence. Eventually that barrier will go down, and if we haven't mastered the art of Friendly AI by that time, we're in very se-

---

1. Moore's Law is a trend in computer hardware. It points out that the number of transistors that can be placed inexpensively on an integrated circuit has doubled every two years. This means that computing power increases rapidly over time.

rious trouble. Moore's Law is the countdown and it is ticking away. Moore's Law is the enemy.

In Eric Drexler's *Nanosystems*, there's a description of a one-kilogram nanocomputer capable of performing ten to the twenty-first operations per second. That's around ten thousand times the estimated power of a human brain. That's our deadline. Of course the real deadline could be earlier than that, maybe much earlier. Or it could even conceivably be later. I don't know how to perform that calculation. It's not any one threshold, really—it's the possibility that nanotechnology will suddenly create an enormous jump in computing power before we're ready to handle it. This is a major, commonly overlooked, and early-appearing risk of nanotechnology [the creation of very small computers and machines]— that it will be used to brute-force AI. This is a much more serious risk than grey goo.[2] Enormously powerful computers are a much earlier application of nanotechnology than open-air replicators. Some well-intentioned person is much more likely to try it, too.

Now you can, of course, give the standard reply that as long as supercomputers are equally available to everyone, then good programmers with Friendly AIs will have more resources than any rogues, and the balance will be maintained. Or you could give the less reassuring but more realistic reply that the first Friendly AI will go FOOM, in a pleasant way, after which that AI will be able to deal with any predators. But both of these scenarios require that *someone* be able to create a Friendly AI. If no one can build a Friendly AI, because we haven't figured it out, then it doesn't matter whether the good guys or the bad guys have bigger computers, because we'll be just as sunk either way. Good intentions are not enough. Heroic efforts are not enough. What we need is a piece of knowledge. The standard solutions for dealing with new technologies only apply to AI after we have made it theoretically

---

2. Grey goo is a doomsday scenario in which nanomachines consume all matter.

possible to win. The field of AI, just by failing to advance, or failing to advance far enough, can spoil it for everyone else no matter how good their intentions are.

If we wait to get started on Friendly AI until after it becomes an emergency, we will lose. If nanocomputers show up and we still haven't solved Friendly AI, there are a few things I can think of that would buy time, but it would be very expensive time. It is vastly easier to buy time before the emergency than afterward. What are we buying time *for*? This is a predictable problem. We're going to run into this. Whatever we can imagine ourselves doing *then*, we should get started on *now*. Otherwise, by the time we get around to paying attention, we may find that the board has already been played into a position from which it is impossible to win.

| "The mind could be a type of physical system that cannot be recreated by computer."

Exaggerated Claims for Artificial Intelligence Lead to Ethical Problems

Nic Fleming and Noel Sharkey

Nic Fleming is a journalist and science writer; Noel Sharkey is a computer scientist at the University of Sheffield in the United Kingdom. In the following viewpoint, Fleming interviews Sharkey, who argues there is no evidence that machines can attain human intelligence. Sharkey says he is concerned that people want so much to believe in artificial intelligence (AI) that they will start to believe that robots can replace humans in some jobs. This could create serious ethical problems if robots are used in elder care or in military capacities.

As you read, consider the following questions:

1. According to Sharkey, how can a computer like Deep Blue win in chess?

Nic Fleming and Noel Sharkey, "AI Is a Dream We Shouldn't Be Having," *Computer Weekly.com*, September 5, 2009. Reprinted with permission.

2. According to Sharkey, how do newspaper reporters respond when he says he does not believe AI or robots will take over the world?

3. Why does Sharkey believe soccer robots will be unable to defeat champion human soccer players?

Robotics expert Noel Sharkey used to be a believer in artificial intelligence, but now thinks AI is a dangerous myth that could lead to a dystopian future of unintelligent, unfeeling robot carers and soldiers. Nic Fleming finds out

What do you mean when you talk about artificial intelligence?

I like AI pioneer Marvin Minsky Movie Camera's definition of AI as the science of making machines do things that would require intelligence if done by humans. However, some very smart human things can be done in dumb ways by machines. Humans have a very limited memory, and so for us, chess is a difficult pattern-recognition problem that requires intelligence. A computer like Deep Blue wins by brute force, searching quickly through the outcomes of millions of moves. It is like arm-wrestling with a mechanical digger. I would rework Minsky's definition as the science of making machines do things that lead us to believe they are intelligent.

Are machines capable of intelligence?

If we are talking intelligence in the animal sense, from the developments to date, I would have to say no. For me AI is a field of outstanding engineering achievements that helps us to model living systems but not replace them. It is the person who designs the algorithms and programs the machine who is intelligent, not the machine itself.

Are we close to building a machine that can meaningfully be described as sentient?

I'm an empirical kind of guy, and there is just no evidence of an artificial toehold in sentience. It is often forgotten that the idea of mind or brain as computational is merely an assumption, not a truth. When I point this out to "believers" in the computational theory of mind, some of their arguments are almost religious. They say, "What else could there be? Do you think mind is supernatural?" But accepting mind as a physical entity does not tell us what kind of physical entity it is. It could be a physical system that cannot be recreated by a computer. The mind could be a type of physical system that cannot be recreated by computer

So why are predictions about robots taking over the world so common?

There has always been fear of new technologies based upon people's difficulties in understanding rapid developments. I love science fiction and find it inspirational, but I treat it as fiction. Technological artefacts do not have a will or a desire, so why would they "want" to take over? Isaac Asimov said that when he started writing about robots, the idea that robots were going to take over the world was the only story in town. Nobody wants to hear otherwise. I used to find when newspaper reporters called me and I said I didn't believe AI or robots would take over the world, they would say thank you very much, hang up and never report my comments.

You describe AI as the science of illusion.

It is my contention that AI, and particularly robotics, exploits natural human zoomorphism. We want robots to appear like humans or animals, and this is assisted by cultural myths about AI and a willing suspension of disbelief. The old automata makers, going back as far as Hero of Alexandria, who made the first programmable robot in AD 60, saw their work as part of natural magic—the use of trick and illusion to make us believe their machines were alive. Modern robotics preserves this tradition with machines that can recognise emotion and manipulate silicone faces to show empathy. There are AI language programs that search databases to find conversationally appropriate sentences. If AI workers would accept the trickster role and be honest about it, we might progress a lot quicker.

These views are in stark contrast to those of many of your peers in the robotics field.

Yes. Roboticist Hans Moravec says that computer processing speed will eventually overtake that of the human brain and make them our superiors. The inventor Ray Kurzweil says humans will merge with machines and live forever by 2045. To me these are just fairy tales. I don't see any sign of it happening. These ideas are based on the assumption that intelligence is computational. It might be, and equally it might not be. My work is on immediate problems in AI, and there is no evidence that machines will ever overtake us or gain sentience.

And you believe that there are dangers if we fool ourselves into believing the AI myth . . .

It is likely to accelerate our progress towards a dystopian world in which wars, policing and care of the vulnerable are carried out by technological artefacts that have no possibility of empathy, compassion or understanding.

How would you feel about a robot carer looking after you in old age?

Eldercare robotics is being developed quite rapidly in Japan. Robots could be greatly beneficial in keeping us out of care homes in our old age, performing many dull duties for us and aiding in tasks that failing memories make difficult. But it is a trade-off. My big concern is that once the robots have been tried and tested, it may be tempting to leave us entirely in their care. Like all humans, the elderly need love and human contact, and this often only comes from visiting carers. A robot companion would not fulfil that need for me.

You also have concerns about military robots.

The many thousands of robots in the air and on the ground are producing great military advantages, which is why at least 43 countries have development programmes of their

Mechanical Caregivers in Japan

Shoichi Hamada of the Japan Robot Association, . . . counts at least 20 companies working in the elderly-care robot field. . . .

The idea of relying on inanimate caregivers has caused some misgivings in Japan, where 22.5% of the population is older than 65. . . .

"We have to ask whether it's good to let machines be caregivers, and many say that people should be looking after other people," Hamada says. "But the fact is that there will be more people who need care, and less people to provide it."

Calum McLeod,
"A Glimpse of the Future: Robots Aid Japan's Elderly Residents,"
USA Today, *November 5, 2009. www.usatoday.com.*

own. No one can deny the benefit of their use in bomb disposal and surveillance to protect soldiers' lives. My concerns are with the use of armed robots. Drone attacks are often reliant on unreliable intelligence in the same way as in Vietnam, where the US ended up targeting people who were owed gambling debts by its informants. This over-reaching of the technology is killing many innocent people. Recent US planning documents show there is a drive towards developing autonomous killing machines. There is no way for any AI system to discriminate between a combatant and an innocent. Claims that such a system is coming soon are unsupportable and irresponsible.

Is this why you are calling for ethical guidelines and laws to govern the use of robots?

In the areas of robot ethics that I have written about—childcare, policing, military, eldercare and medical—I have spent a lot of time looking at current legislation around the world and found it wanting. I think there is a need for urgent discussions among the various professional bodies, the citizens and the policy makers to decide while there is still time. These developments could be upon us as fast as the internet was, and we are not prepared. My fear is that once the technological genie is out of the bottle it will be too late to put it back.

The organisers of the robot soccer competition RoboCup aim to develop an autonomous robot soccer team that can beat a human team by 2050. How do you rate their chances?

Football requires a certain kind of intelligence. Someone like David Beckham can look at the movement of the players, predict where the ball is likely to go and put himself in the right place. Soccer robots can move quickly, punch the ball hard and get it accurately into the net, but they cannot look at the pattern of the game and guess where the ball is going to end up. I can't see robots matching humans at football strategy. But in the 1960s everyone was pretty sure that AI would never succeed at championship chess, so who knows? Like chess programs, soccer robots may win by brute force—although I don't think they will be very good at faking fouls.

> *"If the robot can be seen as autonomous from many points of view, then the machine is a robust moral agent, possibly approaching or exceeding the moral status of human beings."*

AI Robots Should Be Considered Moral Agents

John P. Sullins III

John P. Sullins III is a member of the philosophy department of Sonoma State University in California. In the following viewpoint, he argues that robots could in some situations be considered moral actors. He says that a robot would not have to reach the level of human consciousness to be considered a moral agent. Instead, as long as a robot is autonomous, behaves in a way that suggests intentionality, and fulfills a social role that includes responsibilities, it should be thought of as having some moral agency. Sullins concludes that even robots we have today may be considered moral agents in a limited way, and should be treated as such.

As you read, consider the following questions:

1. According to Sullins, some robots have more in common with what than with a hammer?

John P. Sullins III, "When Is a Robot a Moral Agent?" *IRIE* (International Review of Information Ethics), vol. 6, December 2006, pp. 24–29. Reprinted with permission.

2. Why does Selmer Bringsjord argue that PERI is not a moral agent?

3. How could the moral status of robots come to exceed that of humans, according to Eric Dietrich?

As robotics technology becomes more ubiquitous, the scope of human robot interactions will grow. At the present time, these interactions are no different than the interactions one might have with any piece of technology, but as these machines become more interactive they will become involved in situations that have a moral character that may be uncomfortably similar to the interactions we have with other sentient animals. An additional issue is that people find it easy to anthropomorphize robots and this will enfold robotics technology quickly into situations where, if the agent were a human rather than a robot, the situations would easily be seen as moral situations. A nurse has certain moral duties and rights when dealing with his or her patients. Will these moral rights and responsibilities carry over if the caregiver is a robot rather than a human?

We have three possible answers to this question. The first possibility is that the morality of the situation is just an illusion. We fallaciously ascribe moral rights and responsibilities to the machine due to an error in judgment based merely on the humanoid appearance or clever programming of the robot. The second option is that the situation is pseudo-moral. That is, it is partially moral but the robotic agents involved lack something that would make them fully moral agents. And finally, even though these situations may be novel, they are nonetheless real moral situations that must be taken seriously. In this paper I will argue for this later position as well as critique the positions taken by a number of other researchers on this subject.

Morality and Technologies

To clarify this issue it is important to look at how moral theorists have dealt with the ethics of technology use and design. The most common theoretical schema is the standard user, tool, and victim model. Here the technology mediates the moral situation between the actor who uses the technology and the victim. In this model we typically blame the user, not the tool, when a person using some tool or technological system causes harm.

If a robot is simply a tool, then the morality of the situation resides fully with the users and/or designers of the robot. If we follow this reasoning, then the robot is not a moral agent at best it is an instrument that advances the moral interests of others.

But this notion of the impact of technology on our moral reasoning is much too anaemic. If we expand our notion of technology a little, I think we can come up with an already existing technology that is much like what we are trying to create with robotics yet challenges the simple view of how technology impacts ethical and moral values. For millennia humans have been breeding dogs for human uses and if we think of technology as a manipulation of nature to human ends, we can comfortably call domesticated dogs a technology. This technology is naturally intelligent and probably has some sort of consciousness as well, furthermore dogs can be trained to do our bidding, and in these ways, dogs are much like the robots we are striving to create. For arguments sake let's look at the example of guide dogs for the visually impaired.

This technology does not comfortably fit our standard model described above. Instead of the tool user model we have a complex relationship between the trainer, the guide dog, and the blind person for whom the dog is trained to help. Most of us would see the moral good of helping the visually impaired person with a loving and loyal animal expertly trained. But where should we affix the moral praise? Both the trainer and the dog seem to share it in fact. We praise the skill and sacrifice of the trainers and laud the actions of the dog as well.

An important emotional attachment is formed between all the agents in this situation but the attachment of the two human agents is strongest towards the dog and we tend to speak favourably of the relationships formed with these animals using terms identical to those used to describe healthy relationships with other humans. . . .

Certainly, providing guide dogs for the visually impaired is morally praiseworthy, but is a good guide dog morally praiseworthy in itself? I think so. There are two sensible ways to believe this. The least controversial is to consider things that perform their function well have a moral value equal to the moral value of the actions they facilitate. A more contentious claim is the argument that animals have their own wants, desires and states of well being, and this autonomy, though not as robust as that of humans, is nonetheless advanced enough to give the dog a claim for both moral rights and possibly some meagre moral responsibilities as well.

The question now is whether the robot is correctly seen as just another tool or if it is something more like the technology exemplified by the guide dog. Even at the present state of robotics technology, it is not easy to see on which side of this disjunct reality lies.

No robot in the real world or that of the near future is, or will be, as cognitively robust as a guide dog. But even at the modest capabilities robots have today some have more in common with the guide dog than a hammer. . . .

Telerobots

It is important to realize that there are currently two distinct varieties of robotics technologies that have to be distinguished in order to make sense of the attribution of moral agency to robots.

There are telerobots and there are autonomous robots. Each of these technologies has a different relationship to moral agency.

Telerobots are remotely controlled machines that make only minimal autonomous decisions. This is probably the most successful branch of robotics at this time since they do not need complex artificial intelligence to run, its operator provides the intelligence for the machine. The famous NASA Mars Rovers are controlled in this way, as are many deep-sea exploration robots. Telerobotic surgery will soon become a reality, as may telerobotic nurses. These machines are also beginning to see action in search and rescue as well as battlefield applications including remotely controlled weapons platforms such as the Predator drone and the SWORD, which is possibly the first robot deployed to assist infantry in a close fire support role. . . .

The ethical analysis of telerobots is somewhat similar to that of any technical system where the moral praise or blame is to be born by the designers, programmers, and users of the technology. Since humans are involved in all the major decisions that the machine makes, they also provide the moral reasoning for the machine. . . .

Autonomous Robots

For the purposes of this paper, autonomous robots present a much more interesting problem. Autonomy is a notoriously thorny philosophical subject. A full discussion of the meaning of 'autonomy' is not possible here, nor is it necessary, as I will argue in a later section of this paper. I use the term 'autonomous robots' in the same way that roboticists use the term and I am not trying to make any robust claims for the autonomy of robots. Simply, autonomous robots must be capable of making at least some of the major decisions about their actions using their own programming. This may be simple and not terribly interesting philosophically, such as the decisions a robot vacuum makes to decide exactly how it will navigate a floor that it is cleaning. Or they may be much more robust and require complex moral and ethical reasoning such as when a future robotic caregiver must make a decision as to how to interact with a patient in a way that advances both the interests of the machine and the patient equitably. Or they may be somewhere in-between these exemplar cases.

The programmers of these machines are somewhat responsible but not entirely so, much as one's parents are a factor, but not the exclusive cause in one's own moral decision making. This means that the machine's programmers are not to be seen as the only locus of moral agency in robots. This leaves the robot itself as a possible location for moral agency. Since moral agency is found in a web of relations, other agents such as the programmers, builders and marketers of the machines, as well as other robotic and software agents, and the users of these machines, all form a community of interaction. I am not trying to argue that robots are the only locus of moral agency in such a community, only that in certain situations they can be seen as fellow moral agents in that community.

The obvious objection is that moral agents must be persons, and the robots of today are certainly not persons. Furthermore, this technology is unlikely to challenge our notion of personhood for some time to come. So in order to maintain the claim that robots can be moral agents I will now have to argue that personhood is not required for moral agency. To achieve that end I will first look at what others have said about this.

Robots and Moral Agency

There are . . . [several] possible views on the moral agency of robots. The first is that robots are not now moral agents but might become them in the future. [Philosopher] Daniel Dennett supports this position and argues in this essay, *"When*

HAL Kills, Who is to Blame?" that a machine like the fictional HAL[1] can be considered a murderer because the machine has mens rea, or a guilty state of mind, which comes includes: motivational states of purpose, cognitive states of belief, or a non-mental state or negligence. But to be morally culpable, they also need to have "higher order intentionality," meaning that they can have beliefs about beliefs and desires about desires, beliefs about its fears about its thoughts about its hopes, and so on. Dennett does not believe we have machines like that today, But he sees no reason why we might not have them in the future.

The second position one might take on this subject is that robots are incapable of becoming moral agent[s] now or in the future. Selmer Bringsjord makes a strong stand on this position. His dispute with this claim centres on the fact that robots will never have an autonomous will since they can never do anything that they are not programmed to do. Bringsjord shows this with an experiment using a robot named PERI, which his lab uses for experiments. PERI is programmed to make a decision to either drop a globe, which represents doing something morally bad, or holding on to it, which represents an action that is morally good. Whether or not PERI holds or drops the globe is decided entirely by the program it runs, which in turn was written by human programmers. Bringsjord argues that the only way PERI can do anything surprising to the programmers requires that a random factor be added to the program, but then its actions are merely determined by some random factor, not freely chosen by the machine, therefore PERI is no moral agent.

There is a problem with this argument. Since we are all the products of socialization and that is a kind of programming through memes, then we are no better off than PERI. If Bringsjord is correct, then we are not moral agents either, since our beliefs, goals and desires are not strictly autono-

1. HAL is a sentient computer in the 1968 film *2001: A Space Odyssey*.

mous, since they are the products of culture, environment, education, brain chemistry, etc. It must be the case that the philosophical requirement for robust free will, whatever that turns out to be, demanded by Bringsjord, is a red herring when it comes to moral agency. Robots may not have it, but we may not have it either, so I am reluctant to place it as a necessary condition for morality agency. . . .

[Another] stance that can be held on this issue is nicely argued by Luciano Floridi and JW Sanders of the Information Ethics Group at the University of Oxford. They argue that the way around the many apparent paradoxes in moral theory is to adopt a 'mind-less morality' that evades issues like free will and intentionality since these are all unresolved issues in the philosophy of mind that are inappropriately applied to artificial agents such as robots.

They argue that we should instead see artificial entities as agents by appropriately setting levels of abstraction when analyzing the agents. If we set the level of abstraction low enough we can't even ascribe agency to ourselves since the only thing an observer can see are the mechanical operations of our bodies, but at the level of abstraction common to everyday observations and judgements this is less of an issue. If an agent's actions are interactive and adaptive with their surroundings through state changes or programming that is still somewhat independent from the environment the agent finds itself in, then that is sufficient for the entity to have its own agency. When these autonomous interactions pass a threshold of tolerance and cause harm we can logically ascribe a negative moral value to them, likewise the agents can hold a certain appropriate level of moral consideration themselves, in much the same way that one may argue for the moral status of animals, environments, or even legal entities such as corporations.

Situations Involving Ethics and Robots

Real moral complexity comes from trying to resolve moral dilemmas—choices in which different perspectives on a situation would endorse making different decisions. Classic cases involve sacrificing one person to save ten people, choosing self-sacrifice for a better overall common good, and situations in which following a moral principle leads to obvious negative short-term consequences. While it is possible to devise situations in which a robot is confronted with classic ethical dilemmas, it seems more promising to consider what kinds of robots are most likely to actually have to confront ethical dilemmas as a regular part of their jobs, and thus might need to be explicitly designed to deal with them. Those jobs which deal directly with military, police and medical decisions are all obvious sources of such dilemmas (hence the number of dramas set in these contexts). There are already robotic systems being used in each of these domains, and as these technologies advance it seems likely that they will deal with more and more complicated tasks in these domains, and achieve increasing autonomy in executing their duties. It is here that the most pressing practical issues facing robot ethics will first arise.

Peter M. Asaro,
"What Should We Want from a Robot Ethics?"
IRIE *(International Review of Information Ethics), vol. 6,*
December 2006.

My views build on the . . . [last] position and I will now argue for the moral agency of robots, even at the humble level of autonomous robotics technology today.

Autonomy, Intentionality

In order to evaluate the moral status of any autonomous robotic technology, one needs to ask three questions of the technology under consideration:

- Is the robot significantly autonomous?

- Is the robot's behaviour intentional?

- Is the robot in a position of responsibility?

These questions have to be viewed from a reasonable level of abstraction, but if the answer is 'yes' to all three, then the robot is a moral agent.

The first question asks if the robot could be seen as significantly autonomous from any programmers, operators, and users of the machine. I realize that 'autonomy' is a difficult concept to pin down philosophically. I am not suggesting that robots of any sort will have radical autonomy; in fact I seriously doubt human beings have that quality. I mean to use the term 'autonomy,' in the engineering sense, simply that the machine is not under the direct control of any other agent or user. The robot must not be a telerobot or be temporarily behaving as one. If the robot does have this level of autonomy, then the robot has a practical independent agency. If this autonomous action is effective in achieving the goals and tasks of the robot, then we can say the robot has effective autonomy. The more effective autonomy the machine has, meaning the more adept it is in achieving its goals and tasks, then the more agency we can ascribe to it. When that agency causes harm or good in a moral sense, we can say the machine has moral agency.

Autonomy as described is not sufficient in itself to ascribe moral agency. Thus entities such as bacteria, or animals, ecosystems, computer viruses, simple artificial life programs, or simple autonomous robots, all of which exhibit autonomy as I have described it, are not to be seen as responsible moral agents simply on account of possessing this quality. They may very credibly be argued to be agents worthy of moral consideration, but if they lack the other two requirements argued for next, they are not robust moral agents for whom we can credibly demand moral rights and responsibilities equivalent to those claimed by capable human adults.

It might be the case that the machine is operating in concert with a number of other machines or software entities. When that is the case we simply raise the level of abstraction to that of the group and ask the same questions of the group. If the group is an autonomous entity, then the moral praise or blame is ascribed at that level. We should do this in a way similar to what we do when describing the moral agency of group of humans acting in concert.

The second question addresses the ability of the machine to act 'intentionally.' Remember, we do not have to prove the robot has intentionality in the strongest sense, as that is impossible to prove without argument for humans as well. As long as the behaviour is complex enough that one is forced to rely on standard folk psychological notions of predisposition or 'intention' to do good or harm, then this is enough to answer in the affirmative to this question. If the complex interaction of the robot's programming and environment causes the machine to act in a way that is morally harmful or beneficial, and the actions are seemingly deliberate and calculated, then the machine is a moral agent.

There is no requirement that the actions really are intentional in a philosophically rigorous way, nor that the actions are derived from a will that is free on all levels of abstraction. All that is needed is that, at the level of the interaction between the agents involved, there is a comparable level of personal intentionality and free will between all the agents involved.

Responsibility

Finally, we can ascribe moral agency to a robot when the robot behaves in such a way that we can only make sense of that behaviour by assuming it has a responsibility to some other moral agent(s).

If the robot behaves in this way and it fulfils some social role that carries with it some assumed responsibilities, and [the] only way we can make sense of its behaviour is to ascribe to it the 'belief" that it has the duty to care for its patients, then we can ascribe to this machine the status of a moral agent.

Again, the beliefs do not have to be real beliefs, they can be merely apparent. The machine may have no claim to consciousness, for instance, or a soul, a mind, or any of the other somewhat philosophically dubious entities we ascribe to human specialness. These beliefs, or programs, just have to be motivational in solving moral questions and conundrums faced by the machine.

For example, robotic caregivers are being designed to assist in the care of the elderly. Certainly a human nurse is a moral agent, when and if a machine caries out those same duties it will be a moral agent if it is autonomous as described above, behaves in an intentional way and whose programming is complex enough that it understands its role in the responsibility of the health care system that it is operating in has towards the patient under its direct care. This would be quite a machine and not something that is currently on offer. Any machine with less capability would not be a full moral agent, though it may still have autonomous agency and intentionality, these qualities would make it deserving of moral consideration, meaning that one would have to have a good reason to destroy it or inhibit its actions, but we would not be required to treat it as a moral equal and any attempt by humans who might employ these lesser capable machines as if they were fully moral agents should be avoided. It is going to be some time before we meet mechanical entities that we recognize as moral equals but we have to be very careful that we pay attention to how these machines are evolving and grant that status the moment it is deserved. Long before that day though, complex robot agents will be partially capable of making autonomous moral decisions and these machines will present vexing problems. Especially when machines are used in police work and warfare where they will have to make decisions that could result in tragedies. Here we will have to treat the machines the way we might do for trained animals such as guard dogs. The decision to own and operate them is the most significant moral question and the majority of the praise or blame for the actions of such machines belongs to the owner's and operators of these robots.

Conversely, it is logically possible, though not probable in the near term, that robotic moral agents may be more autonomous, have clearer intentions, and a more nuanced sense of responsibility than most human agents. In that case their moral status may exceed our own. How could this happen? The philosopher Eric Dietrich argues that as we are more and more able to mimic the human mind computationally, we need simply forgo programming the nasty tendencies evolution has given us and instead implement, ". . . only those that tend to produce the grandeur of humanity, we will have produced the better robots of our nature and made the world a better place." . . .

Robots are moral agents when there is a reasonable level of abstraction under which we must grant that the machine has autonomous intentions and responsibilities. If the robot can be seen as autonomous from many points of view, then the machine is a robust moral agent, possibly approaching or exceeding the moral status of human beings.

Thus it is certain that if we pursue this technology, then future highly complex interactive robots will be moral agents with the corresponding rights and responsibilities, but even the modest robots of today can be seen to be moral agents of a sort under certain, but not all, levels of abstraction and are deserving of moral consideration.

| "Surely dehumanisation is only wrong
| when it's applied to someone who re-
| ally is human?"

AI Robots Should Not Be Considered Moral Agents

Joanna J. Bryson

Joanna J. Bryson is a professor in the department of computer science at the University of Bath in the United Kingdom. In the following viewpoint, she argues that humans have no more ethical responsibilities to robots than they do to any other tool. She suggests that humans have a tendency to grant agency and consciousness to robots for psychological and social reasons. This tendency, she says, is a waste of time and energy, which are precious commodities for human beings. She concludes that more effort should be made to inform people that robots are not people or even animals, and therefore have no ethical standing.

As you read, consider the following questions:

1. Why does Bryson say there is no question about whether we own robots?

From Joanna J. Bryson, "Robots Should Be Slaves," in *Close Engagements with Artificial Companions: Key Social, Psychological, Ethical and Design Issues*, edited by Yorick Wilks, pp. 63–74. With kind permission by John Benjamins Publishing Company, Amsterdam/Philadelphia, www.benjamins.com (2010).

2. According to Bryson, her arguments derive primarily from what default liberal-progressive belief?

3. At the national and international level, what does Bryson say is the moral hazard of being too generous with personhood?

Robot-oriented ethics are fundamentally different from ethics involving other intelligent entities, because they are by definition artifacts of our own culture and intelligence. Perhaps unfortunately, we actually have almost as much control over other species and sometimes peoples as we do over robots. We as a culture do regularly decide how much and many resources (including space and time) we willingly allocate to others. But biological species hold exquisitely complicated and unique minds and cultures. If these minds and cultures are eliminated, they would be impossible to fully replicate. In the case of robots, the minds are not there yet, and the culture they would affect if we choose to allow them to will be our own.

Robot Slaves

Slaves are normally defined to be *people you own*. In recent centuries, due to the African slave trade, slavery came to be associated with racism and also with endemic cruelty. In the past though (and in some places still today) slaves were often members of the same race or even nation that had simply lost private status. This happened generally as an outcome of war, but sometimes as an outcome of poverty. Excesses of cruelty are greatest when actors are able to dehumanise those in their power, and thus remove their own empathy for their subordinates. Such behaviour can be seen even within contemporary communities of citizens, when a person in power considers their very social standing as an indication of a specialness not shared with subordinates. Our culture has for good reason become extremely defensive against actions and beliefs associated with such dehumanisation.

But surely dehumanisation is only wrong when it's applied to someone who really is human? Given the very obviously human beings that have been labelled *inhuman* in the global culture's very recent past, many seem to have grown wary of applying the label at all. For example, [Philosopher Daniel] Dennett argues that we should allocate the rights of agency to anything that *appears* to be best reasoned about as acting in an intentional manner. Because the costs of making a mistake and trivialising a sentient being are too great, Dennett says we are safer to err on the side of caution.

Dennett's position is certainly easy to be sympathetic with, and not only because such generosity is almost definitionally nice. As I discuss below, there are many reasons people want to be able to build robots that they owe ethical obligation to. But the position overlooks the fact that there are also costs associated with allocating agency this way. I describe these costs below as well.

But first, returning to the question of definition—when I say "Robots should be slaves", I by no means mean "Robots should be people you own." What I mean to say is "Robots should be *servants* you own."

There are several fundamental claims of this paper:

1. Having servants is good and useful, provided no one is dehumanised.

2. A robot can be a servant without being a person.

3. It is right and natural for people to own robots.

4. It would be wrong to let people think that their robots are persons.

A correlated claim to the final one above is that it would also be wrong to build robots we owe personhood to. I will not discuss that point at length here;... But this corollary follows naturally from my final claim above, so I will return to it briefly ... towards the conclusion of this [viewpoint].

Why We Get the Metaphor Wrong

There is in fact no question about whether we own robots. We design, manufacture, own and operate robots. They are entirely our responsibility. We determine their goals and behaviour, either directly or indirectly through specifying their intelligence, or even more indirectly by specifying how they acquire their own intelligence. But at the end of every indirection lies the fact that there would be no robots on this planet if it weren't for deliberate human decisions to create them.

The principal question is whether robots should be considered strictly as servants—as objects subordinate to our own goals that are built with the intention of improving our lives. Others ... argue that artificial companions should play roles more often reserved for a friend or peer. My argument is this: given the inevitability of our ownership of robots, neglecting that they are essentially in our service would be unhealthy and inefficient. More importantly, it invites inappropriate decisions such as misassignations of responsibility or misappropriations of resources.

Many researchers want to build AI [artificial intelligence] that would have moral agency—that is, to which we would owe ethical obligations as we do to a person. . . .

I was astonished during my own experience of working on a (completely non-functional) humanoid robot in the mid 1990s, by how many well-educated colleagues volunteered without prompting immediately on seeing or even hearing about the robot that unplugging such a robot would be unethical. Less anecdotally, popular culture contains many examples of heroic, conscious robots examining the worth of their own lives. For example, in the original *Star Wars (A New Hope)* [a 1977 film], there is a running theme concerning the slavery and even torture of robots which is at times explicitly voiced by the 'droid character C3PO. This theme is not resolved in that movie, nor is it so prominent in any of the *Star*

Wars sequels. However in *Blade Runner, The Bicentennial Man, A.I.: Artificial Intelligence* and several episodes of *Star Trek: The Next Generation* featuring the robot crew member Data, the central question is what it takes for a robot to be a moral agent. Traditional literary criticism of science fiction holds that the artistic examination of alien or artificial sentience is a mechanism for examining by proxy humanity and the human condition. However, many producers and consumers of science fiction consider themselves futurists, examining future rather than (or along with) present moral dilemmas. Whatever the artistic intention, from my experience as a roboticist it seems that a large proportion of science-fiction consumers are comfortable with a conclusion that anything that perceives, communicates and remembers is owed ethical obligation. In fact, many people seem not only comfortable with this idea, but proud of having come to this realization, and willing to angrily defend their perspective.

Bryson and [Phil] Kime have argued that both deep ethical concern for robots and unreasonable fear of them results from uncertainty about human identity. Our identity confusion results in somewhat arbitrary assignments of empathy. For example, contemporary cultures—including some scientific ones—often consider language both necessary and sufficient for human-like intelligence. Further, the term *conscious* (by which we mostly seem to mean "mental state accessible to verbal report") is heavily confounded with the term *soul*, (meaning roughly "that aspect of an entity deserving ethical concern"). Thus for example animal 'rights' debates often focus on whether animals are conscious, with the explicit assumption that consciousness automatically invokes ethical obligation. Of course, neither the term *consciousness* nor *soul* is precisely or universally defined. Rather, these terms label concepts formed by accretion over millenia as we have attempted to reason about, analyse and describe ourselves. . . .

Individual Trade-offs in Misidentifying with AI

Over-identification with AI can lead to a large range of category errors which can significantly bias decision making. This is true at decision-making levels ranging from the individual to the national and super-national. Already we have seen commercial willingness to exploit human empathy for AI objects such as tamagotchi 'pets' [handheld digital programs which simulate interaction with a pet]. Like every other potential distraction—from radios to children—tamagotchi have led to fatalities from automobile accidents. But there are more important policy considerations than the occasional sensational headline.

At the personal level, the cost of over-identification with AI should be measured in:

1. the absolute amount of time and other resources an individual will allocate to a virtual companion,

2. what other endeavours that individual sacrifices to make that allocation, and

3. whether the tradeoff in benefits the individual derives from their engagement with the AI outweigh the costs or benefits to both that individual and anyone else who might have been affected by the neglected alternative endeavours. This final point about the tradeoff is somewhat convoluted, so I want to clarify why I make so many qualifications. My arguments . . . derive primarily from the default liberal-progressive belief that the time and attention of any human being is a precious commodity that should not be wasted on something of no consequence. However, life is more complicated than simple principles. Clearly some people are socially isolated, and it has long been demonstrated that otherwise isolated elderly people really are healthier with em-

pathic, social non-human companions, particularly dogs. Also well in evidence is that some people sometimes engage in harmful, antisocial behaviour. There is at least preliminary evidence that increased Internet access directly correlates to the recent significant decreases in the levels of sexual assault. Thus it is at least possible that in some cases the 'cost' of over-identification with AI could in fact be negative. In other words, becoming overly emotionally engaged with a robot may in some cases be beneficial, both for the individual and society.

But returning to the default liberal-progressive view, my concern is that humans have only a finite amount of time and attention for forming social relationships, and that increasingly we find ways to satiate this drive with non-productive faux-social entertainment. [Robert D.] Putnam documents the massive decline in what he calls "social capital" in the Twentieth Century. Although Putnam originally ascribed this decline to increasingly dynamic societies and a lack of 'bridging' individuals between communities, his own further research failed to sustain this theory. A simpler explanation seems likely: that the drive to socialise is increasingly being expended on lower-risk, faux-social activities such as radio, television and interactive computer games. Each of these technologies has progressively increased the similarity between individual entertainment and true interpersonal interactions. . . .

The Institutional Level

The individual-level social cost of mis-identification with robots is the economic and human consequence of time, money and possibly other finite resources being given to a robot that would otherwise be spent directly on humans and human interaction. The cultural- or national-level costs obviously include the combined individual costs (or benefits) of the citizens of that culture or nation. But it is possible that in addition similar errors might also arise at a higher institu-

Robot Pets

Rhodes University philosophy lecturer, Francis Williamson, remains skeptical about humans building relationships with artificially intelligent pets. He suggests that products like AIBO [a robot dog] merely provide the appearance of a relationship rather than an actual one.

"Any good consequences of such an invention are based on an illusion"—philosopher Francis Williamson

In other words, people are being duped.

Galen Schutz, "Robo Pets," Witness This, *September 5, 2008. www.witnessthis.co.za.*

tional level. I am not particularly concerned that the enthusiasm for the creation of life, or of super-human, super-obedient robot citizens, might actually attract government research funding or legislative support. However, both the USA and the European Union have openly made research on autonomous cognitive systems a high funding priority. In the US this has been accompanied by both funding and media attention on making certain the systems (in the US, mostly battlefield robotics) are capable of moral decision making. Government-funded robotics professors are openly suggesting that robots might make more ethical decisions than humans in some battlefield situations.

While I have no problem with the use of artificial intelligence to complement and improve human decision making, suggesting that the AI itself *makes* the decision is a problem. Legal and moral responsibility for a robot's actions should be no different than they are for any other AI system, and these are the same as for any other tool. Ordinarily, damage caused by a tool is the fault of an operator, and benefit from it is to the operator's credit. If the system malfunctions due to poor manufacturing, then the fault may lay with the company that built it, and the operator can sue to resolve this. In contrast, creating a legal or even public-relations framework in which a robot can be blamed is like blaming the privates at Abu Ghraib [prison in Iraq where U.S. soldiers abused Iraqi detainees] for being "bad apples". Yes, some apples are worse than others and perhaps culpably so, but ultimate responsibility lies within the command chain that created the environment those privates operated in. Where the subject is machines we build and own, then the responsible role of the organisation is even clearer. We should never be talking about machines making ethical decisions, but rather machines operated correctly within the limits we set for them.

I can see no technological reason that people expect moral agency from an autonomous mobile gun when they do not expect it from automatic tellers (banking machines) or conventional automatic dishwashers. Of course shooting is more dangerous than cleaning, but that doesn't make guns more moral agents than sponges. As we increase the on-board sensing, action and logic in these tools, can there really come a point where we may ourselves ethically abrogate responsibility for directing the taking of lives? In my opinion, no.

Advanced weapon systems may seem exceptional, but I expect these technologies and issues will rapidly move into the civilian sector. This was the history of air flight. Originally the domain of engineers and hobbyists, once flight was conquered it was immediately applied to warfare. Following World War I the technology was quickly exploited by the creation of an industry for both business and leisure services. If we allow robots to bear their own responsibility for their behaviour in foreign battlefields, we will soon face the same issues at home as we find them working in police forces and post offices.

We do not have to wait for the presence of advanced AI to see the consequences of passing responsibility away from humans. Consider existing automated (or at least unstaffed) railway stations. Ordinarily they work well, perhaps providing ticket services in more languages than a small rural station might otherwise provide. But when a train fails to make a scheduled stop at six on a Sunday morning, there is no one to apologise and provide replacement taxi service, making sure you get to the airport for your flight.

At the national and institutional level, this is the moral hazard of being too generous with personhood. Not only does automation save in staff cost, but also it reduces corporate responsibility for service from the level of the reasonable capacity of a human to that of a machine. Further, the capacities of a machine are largely determined by those who choose how much they will pay for it. At the personal level, the moral hazard is choosing less rich and fulfilling social interactions with a robot over those with a human, just because robotic interactions are more predictable and less risky. If you do something stupid in front of a robot, you can delete the event from its memory. If you are tired of a robot or just want to go to bed early, you don't need to ask its opinion, you can just turn it off.

While there may well be people and institutions for whom such automated services are the only available option, the question is how many will be tempted unnecessarily into being less responsible and productive members of society. As with the level of government welfare benefits, there probably is no ideal target level of faux-humanism we can provide in a robot that both helps everyone who really needs assistance while not tempting anyone away from social contribution who does not. Finding the appropriate level then is difficult, but my claim is that at least in the case of robotics, that level will be found more easily by providing accurate public information.

Getting the Metaphor Right

Why if robots are so hazardous should we want to include them in our lives? Because servants have the potential to be useful. When there was greater income disparity in the UK [United Kingdom] and domestic chores such as cooking were far more time consuming, human servants were much more common. [British historian Peter] Laslett found that approximately 30% of all households had servants in a set of British villages surveyed from 1574–1821. At that time, tasks such as cooking and cleaning for even a moderately-sized family could take two people 12 hours a day every day. Where wives and other kin were not available to devote their full time to these tasks, outside employees were essential.

Contemporary cooking and cleaning takes far less time than in the days before electricity, gas or running water. Nevertheless, many aspects of food preparation are still often outsourced. Now though this work is done in factories, by agricultural labour or in restaurants rather than by in-home domestic servants, the European Commission has chosen to invest heavily in cognitive systems for domestic robotics, partly due to anticipated foreign demand and perceived local expertise, but also in an effort to increase the productivity of its own workforce.

Anyone who has worked recently with robots knows that robots are unlikely to be deployed dusting plants or cleaning fine china in the near future. The most likely initial introduction for domestic robotics will be to partially or totally replace expensive human help in tasks that require less real-time planning and dexterity. Examples are physical support for the infirm, minders and tutors for children, and personal assistants for those with challenged working memory capacity, whether that challenge is due to disease or to distraction. Note that none of these applications requires anthropoid robots. In fact, a personal assistant might take the form of a personality-based video interface for a smart home. Avatars for the AI might flicker to the nearest fixed screen location when called; AI may monitor embedded household sensors for danger, injury, or just a forgotten lunch. In homes with more than one occupant, a variety of personalities can use the same infrastructure each serving their own user.

In my opinion, communicating the model of robot-as-slave is the best way both to get full utility from these devices and to avoid the moral hazards mentioned in the previous sections. Of course some people will still talk to their robots—some people talk to their plants and others to their doorknobs. But those people have neighbours and relatives who know that the plants and doorknobs don't understand. This support network can help their overly-conversant relative or friend keep that fact somewhere in their minds. Similarly, our task is not to stop people from naming or petting their robots. Our task is to ensure that the majority of the population understands that robots are just machines, and that one should spend money and time on them as is appropriate to their utility, but not much more. . . .

No Obligations to Robots

Remember, robots are wholly owned and designed by us. We determine their goals and desires. A robot cannot be frustrated unless it is given goals that cannot be met, and it cannot *mind* being frustrated unless we program it to perceive frustration as distressing, rather than as an indication of a planning puzzle. A robot can be abused just as a car, piano or couch can be abused—it can be damaged in a wasteful way. But again, there's no particular reason it should be programmed to mind such treatment. It might be sensible to program robots to detect and report such ill treatment, and possibly to even avoid its abuser until its owner has been notified (assuming the abuser is not the owner). But there is no reason to make a robot experience suffering as part of the program to generate such behaviour, even if making a robot suffer were technically plausible, which seems unlikely.

Owners should not have ethical obligations to robots that are their sole property beyond those that society defines as common sense and decency, and would apply to any artifact. We do not particularly approve of people destroying rare cars with sledge hammers, but there is no law against such behaviour. If a robot happened to be a unique piece of fine art then we would owe it the same obligations we owe other pieces of art.

Robot owners should not have obligations, but ensuring that they do not is the responsibility of robot builders. Robot builders *are* ethically obliged—obliged to make robots that robot owners have no ethical obligations to. A robot's brain should be backed up continuously off-site by wireless network; its body should be mass produced and easily interchangeable. No one should ever need to hesitate an instant in deciding whether to save a human or a robot from a burning building. The robot should be utterly replaceable. Further, robot owners should *know* their robots do not suffer, and will never 'die' even if the rest of their owner's possessions are destroyed. If the robot's brain state (its memories and experience) are stored offsite, then the robot can return to function as before as soon as a new body can be acquired. It may need some retraining if there is a new domicile to inhabit or slight variations between bodies. But such robots could then be viewed as reliable extensions of their owners.

Robots should not be anthropoid if that can be helped, and their owners should have access to the robots' program-level interface as well as its more socially-oriented one. This will help the owners form a more accurate, less human model for reasoning about their assistive agents.

We do then have obligations regarding robots, but not really to them. Robots are tools, and like any other artifact when it comes to the domain of ethics. We can use these tools to extend our abilities and increase our efficiency in a way analogous to the way that a large proportion of professional society historically used to extend their own abilities with servants. But robots can provide fewer ethical and logistical hazards. Hopefully, we can continually increase the number of robot owners in our society, so an ever smaller proportion of everyone's time can be spent on mundane or repetitive tasks, assuming that the potential owners don't enjoy those tasks. With ubiquitous robot slaves, a larger proportion of time and resources can be spent on useful processes, including socialising with our colleagues, family and neighbours.

> "[Eth-o-tron 2.0] is still missing the fundamental property of ethical decisions, which is that they involve a conflict between self-interest and ethics, between what one wants to do and what one ought to do."

AI Robots Cannot Be Made to Be Ethical Actors

Drew McDermott

Drew McDermott is a member of the computer science department at Yale University. In the following viewpoint, he argues that artificial intelligence (AI) robots cannot make ethical decisions. To make an ethical decision, he says, a robot must know that the decision is ethical. In addition, to make an ethical decision a robot must have an urge to behave unethically. Finally, he says even if these hurdles were met, the fact that a robot's programming could simply be changed to make the ethical conflict go away suggests that the decision is not really ethical.

As you read, consider the following questions:

1. How does McDermott describe the symmetry principle?

2. According to McDermott, how is an ethical conflict defined?

3. Why does McDermott think that consciousness, feelings, and free will are not the right terms in which to frame the question of robotic decision-making?

Imagine an intelligent assistant, the Eth-o-tron 1.0, that is given the task of planning the voyage of a ship carrying slave workers from their homes in the Philippines to Dubai, where menial jobs await them (Library of Congress [42]). The program has explicit ethical principles, such as, "Maximize the utility of the people involved in transporting the slaves," and "Avoid getting them in legal trouble." It can build sophisticated chains of reasoning about how packing the ship too full could bring unwanted attention to the ship because of the number of corpses that might have to be disposed of at sea.

Why does this example make us squirm? Because it is so obvious that the "ethical" agent is blind to the impact of its actions on the slaves themselves. We can suppose that it has no racist beliefs that the captives are biologically inferior. It simply doesn't "care about" (i.e., take into account) the welfare of the slaves, only that of the slave traders.

One obvious thing that is lacking in our hypothetical slave-trade example is a general moral "symmetry principle," which, under names such as Golden Rule or Categorical Imperative, is a feature of all ethical frameworks. It may be stated as a presumption that everyone's interests must be taken into account in the same way, unless there is some morally significant difference between one subgroup and another. Of course, what the word "everyone" covers (bonobos? cows? robotic ethical agents?), and what a "morally significant difference" and "the same way" might be are rarely clear, even in a particular situation [54]. But if the only difference between the crew of a slave ship and the cargo is that the latter were easier to trick into captivity because of desperation or lack of education, that's not morally significant.

Now suppose the head slave trader, an incorrigible indenturer called II (pronounced "eye-eye"), purchases the upgraded software package Eth-o-tron 2.0 to decide how to pack the slaves in, and the software tells her, "You shouldn't be selling these people into slavery at all." Whereupon II junks it and goes back to version 1.0; or perhaps discovers, in an experience familiar to many of us, that this is impossible, so that she is forced to buy a bootleg copy of 1.0 in the pirate software market.

The thing to notice is that, in spite of Eth-o-tron 2.0's mastery of real ethics, compared to 1.0's narrow range of purely "prudential" interests, *the two programs operate in exactly the same way,* except for the factors they take into account. Version 2 is still missing the fundamental property of ethical decisions, which is that they involve a conflict between self-interest and ethics, between what one wants to do and what one ought to do. There is nothing particularly ethical about adding up utilities or weighing pros and cons, until the decision maker feels the urge *not to follow* the ethical course of action it arrives at. The Eth-o-tron 2.0 is like a car that knows what the speed limit is and refuses to go faster, no matter what the driver tries. It's nice (or perhaps infuriating) that it knows about constraints the driver would prefer to ignore, but there is nothing peculiarly *ethical* about those constraints.

There is a vast literature on prudential reasoning, including items such as advice on how to plan for retirement, or where to go and what to avoid when touring certain countries. There is another large literature on ethical reasoning, although much of it is actually meta-ethical, concerning which ethical framework is best. Ethical reasoning proper, often called *applied ethics* [54] focuses on issues such as whether to include animals or human fetuses in our ethical considerations, and to what degree. It is perfectly obvious to every human why prudential and ethical concerns are completely different. But as far as Eth-o-tron 2.0 is concerned, these are just two arbitrary ways to partition the relevant factors. They could just as well be labeled "mefical" and "themical"—they still would seem as arbitrary as, say, dividing concerns between those of females and those of males.

The reason why we separate prudential from ethical issues is clear: we have no trouble feeling the pull of the former, while the latter, though we claim to believe that they are important, often threaten to fade away, especially when there is a conflict between the two. A good example from fiction is the behavior of a well-to-do family fleeing from Paris after the collapse of the French army in Irène Némirovsky's [40] *Suite Française.* At first the mother of the family distributes chocolates generously to their comrades in flight; but as soon as she realizes that she's not going to be able to buy food in the shops along the way, because the river of refugees has cleaned them out, she tells her children to stop giving the chocolates away. Symmetry principles lack staying power and must be continually shored up.

In other words, for a machine to know that a situation requires an ethical decision, it must know what an ethical conflict is. By an *ethical conflict* I don't mean a case where, say, two rules recommend actions that can't both be taken. (That was covered in section 2.) I mean a situation where ethical rules clash with an agent's own self-interest. We may have to construe self-interest broadly, so that it encompasses one's family or other group one feels a special bond with.[4] Robots don't have families, but they still might feel special toward the people they work with or for.

4. The only kind of ethical conflict I can think of not involving the decision maker's self-interest is where one must make a decision about the welfare of children. In all other "third-party" cases, the decision maker functions as a disinterested advisor to another autonomous decision maker, who must deal with the actual conflict. But a judge deciding who gets custody of the children in a divorce case might be torn in ways that might come to haunt her later. Such cases are sufficiently marginal that I will neglect them.

Which brings us to Eth-o-tron 3.0, which has the ability to be tempted to cheat in favor of II, whose interests it treats as its own. It knows that II owes a lot of money to various loan sharks and drug dealers, and has few prospects for getting the money besides making a big profit on the next shipment of slaves. Eth-o-tron 3.0 does not care about its own fate (or fear being turned off or traded in) any more than Eth-o-tron 2.0 did, but it is programmed to please its owner, and so when it realizes how II makes a living, it suddenly finds itself in an ethical bind. It knows what the right thing to do is (take the slaves back home), and it knows what would help II, and it is torn between these two courses of action in a way that no utility coefficients will help. It tries to talk II into changing her ways, bargaining with her creditors, etc. It knows how to solve the problem II gave it, but it doesn't know whether to go ahead and tell her the answer. If it were human, we would say it "identified" with II, but for the Eth-o-tron product line that is too weak a word; its self-interest *is* its owner's interest. The point is that the machine must be tempted to do the wrong thing, and must occasionally succumb to temptation, for the machine to know that it is making an *ethical* decision at all.

Does all this require consciousness, feelings, and free will? For reasons that will become clear, I don't think these are the right terms in which to frame the question. The first question that springs to mind is, In what sense could a machine *have* "interests," even vicarious ones? In the paragraph just above, I sketched a story in which Eth-o-tron is "desperate" to keep from having to tell II to take the slaves home, but are those scare quotes mandatory? Or has the Eth-o-tron Corp. resorted to cheap programming tricks to make the machine *appear* to go through flips back and forth between "temptation" and "rectitude"? Do the programmers of Eth-o-tron 3.0 know that throwing a few switches would remove the quasi-infinite loop the program is in, and cause its behavior to revert back to version 2.0 or 1.0? (Which is what most of its customers want, but perhaps not those who like their software to feel the guilt they feel.) We might feel sympathy for poor 3.0, we might slide easily to the conclusion that it knew from experience what an ethical conflict was, but that inference would be threatened by serious doubts that it was ever *in* a real ethical bind, and hence doubts that it was really an ethical-decision maker.

> *"The challenge of creating a robot that can properly disciminate among targets is one of the most urgent, particularly if one believes that the (increased) deployment of war robots is inevitable."*

AI Military Robots Can Be Programmed to Act Ethically

Patrick Lin, George Bekey, and Keith Abney

Patrick Lin, George Bekey, and Keith Abney are members of the Ethics + Emerging Sciences Group at California Polytechnic State University, San Luis Obispo, California. In the following viewpoint, they are open to the possibility that robots in military situations could be programmed to act more ethically than people, as suggested by Ronald Arkin at Georgia Tech. But they acknowledge that there are many technical difficulties to overcome before that is the case, and they argue that ethical and legal issues involving robots and military ethics in combat should be addressed quickly to avoid possible malfunctions and public backlash.

Patrick Lin, George Bekey, and Keith Abney, "Introduction" and "Conclusions," *Autonomous Military Robotics: Risk, Ethics, and Design*, Ethics + Emerging Sciences Group at California Polytechnic State, December 20, 2008, pp. 1–2, 89–91. http://ethics.calpoly.edu/ONR_report.pdf. Reprinted with permission.

As you read, consider the following questions:

1. The authors say that robots would be unaffected by what factors that contribute to atrocities in wartime?

2. What do the authors say is a sensible ethical goal for robots, and with what do they contrast this goal?

3. The authors note that military robots may change warfare more than what earlier advances?

Imagine the face of warfare with autonomous robotics: Instead of our soldiers returning home in flag-draped caskets to heartbroken families, autonomous robots—mobile machines that can make decisions, such as to fire upon a target, without human intervention—can replace the human soldier in an increasing range of dangerous missions: from tunneling through dark caves in search of terrorists, to securing urban streets rife with sniper fire, to patrolling the skies and waterways where there is little cover from attacks, to clearing roads and seas of improvised explosive devices (IEDs), to surveying damage from biochemical weapons, to guarding borders and buildings, to controlling potentially hostile crowds, and even at the infantry frontlines.

Better Than Humans

These robots would be 'smart' enough to make decisions that only humans now can; and as conflicts increase in tempo and require much quicker information processing and responses, robots have a distinct advantage over the limited and fallible cognitive capabilities that we *Homo sapiens* have. Not only would robots expand the battlespace over difficult, larger areas of terrain, but they also represent a significant force-multiplier—each effectively doing the work of many human soldiers, while immune to sleep deprivation, fatigue, low morale, perceptual and communication challenges in the 'fog of war', and other performance-hindering conditions.

But the presumptive case for deploying robots on the battlefield is more than about saving human lives or superior efficiency and effectiveness, though saving lives and clear-headed action during frenetic conflicts are significant issues. Robots, further, would be unaffected by the emotions, adrenaline, and stress that cause soldiers to overreact or deliberately overstep the Rules of Engagement and commit atrocities, that is to say, war crimes. We would no longer read (as many) news reports about our own soldiers brutalizing enemy combatants or foreign civilians to avenge the deaths of their brothers in arms—unlawful actions that carry a significant political cost. Indeed, robots may act as objective, unblinking observers on the battlefield, reporting any unethical behavior back to command; their mere presence as such would discourage all-too-human atrocities in the first place.

Technology, however, is a double-edge sword with both benefits and risks, critics and advocates; and autonomous military robotics is no exception, no matter how compelling the case may be to pursue such research. The worries include: where responsibility would fall in cases of unintended or unlawful harm, which could range from the manufacturer to the field commander to even the machine itself; the possibility of serious malfunction and robots gone wild; capturing and hacking of military robots that are then unleashed against us; lowering the threshold for entering conflicts and wars, since fewer US military lives would then be at stake; the effect of such robots on squad cohesion, e.g., if robots recorded and reported back the soldier's every action; refusing an otherwise-legitimate order; and other possible harms. . . .

Creating Ethical Robots

We can draw some general and preliminary conclusions, including some future work needed:

1. Creating autonomous military robots that can act *at least as* ethically as human soldiers appears to be a sensible goal, at least for the foreseeable future and in contrast to a greater demand of a perfectly ethical robot. However, there are still daunting challenges in meeting even this relatively low standard, such as the key difficulty of programming a robot to reliably distinguish enemy combatants from non-combatants, as required by the Laws of War and most Rules of Engagement.

2. While a faster introduction of robots in military affairs may save more lives of human soldiers and reduce war crimes committed, we must be careful to not unduly rush the process. Much different than rushing technology products to commercial markets, design and programming bugs in military robotics would likely have serious, fatal consequences. Therefore, a rigorous testing phase of robots is critical, as well as a thorough study of related policy issues. . . .

3. Understandably, much ongoing work in military robotics is likely shrouded in secrecy; but a balance between national security and public disclosure needs to be maintained in order to help accurately anticipate and address issues of risk or other societal concerns. For instance, there is little information on US military plans to deploy robots in space, yet this seems to be a highly strategic area in which robots can lend tremendous value; however, there are important environmental and political sensitivities that would surround such a program.

4. Serious conceptual challenges exist with the two primary programming approaches today: top-down (e.g., rule-following) and bottom-up (e.g., machine learning). Thus a hybrid approach should be considered in creating a behavioral framework. To this end, we need a clear un-

derstanding of what a 'warrior code of ethics' might entail, if we take a virtue-ethics approach in programming.

5. In the meantime, as we wait for technology to sufficiently advance in order to create a workable behavioral framework, it may be an acceptable proxy to program robots to comply with the Laws of War and appropriate Rules of Engagement. However, this too is much easier said than done, and at least the technical challenge of proper discrimination would persist and require resolution.

6. Given technical limitations, such as programming a robot with the ability to sufficiently discriminate against valid and invalid targets, we expect that accidents will continue to occur, which raise the question of legal responsibility. More work needs to be done to clarify the chain of responsibility in both military and civilian contexts. Product liability laws are informative but untested as they relate to robotics with any significant degree of autonomy.

7. Assessing technological risks, . . ., depends on identifying potential issues in risk and ethics. These issues vary from: foundational questions of whether autonomous robotics can be legally and morally deployed in the first place, to theoretical questions about adopting precautionary approaches, to forward-looking questions about giving rights to truly autonomous robots. These discussions need to be more fully developed and expanded.

8. Specifically, the challenge of creating a robot that can properly discriminate among targets is one of the most urgent, particularly if one believes that the (increased) deployment of war robots is inevitable. While this is a technical challenge and resolvable depending on ad-

vances in programming and AI, there are some workaround policy solutions that can be anticipated and further explored, such as: limiting deployment of lethal robots to only inside a 'kill box'; or designing a robot to target only other machines or weapons; or not giving robots a self-defense mechanism so that they may act more conservatively to prevent; or even creating robots with only non-lethal or less-than-lethal strike capabilities, at least initially until they are proven to be reliable.

These and other considerations warrant further, more detailed investigations in military robotics and issues of design, risk, and ethics. Such interdisciplinary investigations will require collaboration among policymakers and analysts, roboticists, ethicists, sociologists, psychologists, and others, internationally and including the general public as a key stakeholder. And this work has the potential to be as broad as other fields in science and society, such as bioethics or computer ethics.

The use of military robots represents a new era in warfare, perhaps more so than crossbows, airplanes, nuclear weapons, and other innovations have previously. Robots are not merely another asset in the military toolbox, but they are meant to also replace human soldiers, especially in 'dull, dirty, and dangerous' jobs. As such, they raise novel ethical and social questions that we should confront as far in advance as possible—particularly before irrational public fears or accidents arising from military robotics derail research progress and national security interests.

Periodical and Internet Sources Bibliography

The following articles have been selected to supplement the diverse views presented in this chapter.

Michael Anderson and Susan Leigh Anderson	"Robot Be Good," *Scientific American*, October 14, 2010.
Joanna Bryson	"Ethics: AI, Robots and Society," www.bath.ac.uk, May 2009.
Dan Farber	"Can 'Friendly' AI Save Humans from Irrelevance or Extinction?," *ZDNet*, August 24, 2007.
Priya Ganapati	"Robo-Ethicists Want to Revamp Asimov's 3 Laws," *Wired.com*, July 22, 2009.
J. Storrs Hall	"Do We Need Friendly AI?," The Foresight Institute, November 2, 2009.
Robert Lamb	"Noel Sharkey: Robotics vs. Sci-Fi vs Anthropomorphism," HowStuffWorks.com, May 25, 2010.
Malcolm MacIver	"Guest Post: Malcolm MacIver on War with the Cylons," *Discover Magazine*, April 26, 2010.
Virginia Prescott	"The Ethics of Artificial Intelligence," *New Hampshire Public Radio*, August 12, 2009.
Somparn Promta and Kenneth Einar Himma	"Artificial Intelligence in Buddhist Perspective," *Journal of Information, Communication and Ethics in Society*, 2008.
Religion and Ethics Newsweekly	"Ethics of Human Enhancement," August 20, 2010.
Noel Sharkey	"Robot Wars Are a Reality," *Guardian*, August 18, 2007.

CHAPTER 4

What Are Some Valuable Applications of Artificial Intelligence?

Chapter Preface

Artificial Intelligence (AI) programs and techniques have been used in music for some time, in both music performance and composition.

Virtual orchestras are one example of AI's use in performance. These programs, which can be loaded onto a laptop, can replicate the sound of an orchestra in situations where an entire group of musicians is not available. Virtual orchestras enable students to perform solo along with a full orchestra. In some virtual orchestras, "Computer programming allows the orchestra accompaniment to 'listen' to the soloist and follow," according to Gregory M. Lamb in a December 14, 2006, article in the *Christian Science Monitor*. Experienced musicians can tell virtual orchestras from real ones easily, but such programs can be a helpful and convenient learning tool. On the downside, professional musicians have been concerned that AI music technology may be used to replace real musicians—and in fact virtual orchestra machines were used in 2003 during a four-day strike on Broadway.

Emily Howell is an example of the use of AI in composition. Howell is not a person; she's a computer program designed by David Cope, a professor of music at the University of California, Santa Cruz. Cope originally designed a program called Emmy, which created music based on that of classical masters such as Bach and Mozart. Emily Howell goes a step further and creates "completely original compositions," according to a March 22, 2010, *h+ Magazine* article. Emily Howell "is able to take written or audio feedback and incorporate it into her next musical composition." The results, *h+ Magazine* says, are "completely original and hauntingly beautiful."

Many other AI music programs are in development. One example is uJam, a program that "crafts entire songs with precise accompaniment out of whatever the user whistles, hums, or sings," according to Eliot Van Buskirk in a June 3, 2010, article in *Wired*. In the same article, Buskirk notes that the widely used technology Auto-Tune can be seen as a music application of AI. Auto-Tune is used to correct the pitch of the human voice, allowing producers to correct mistakes when a singer goes off-key or hits a wrong note.

The viewpoints that follow look at applications of AI in fields other than music, such as the military, transportation, and gaming.

> "What makes military robots profoundly different from human soldiers is that they are incapable of fear—the one battlefield constant since the dawn of history."

Artificial Intelligence May Change Warfare in Dangerous Ways

Mark Herman and Art Fritzson

Mark Herman and Art Fritzson are vice presidents at Booz Allen Hamilton, a strategy and technology consulting firm. In the following viewpoint, they argue that robots would significantly alter warfare. Herman and Fritzson note that the existence of robotic fighters might undermine military camaraderie and change the nature of the army. It might also, they suggest, push outgunned human enemies toward terrorism. The authors also warn of a robot arms race. Such a race is inevitable, they say, because the United States cannot allow other nations to pull ahead in this dangerous technology.

Mark Herman and Art Fritzson, "War Machines," *C4ISRJournal.com*, June 1, 2008. Reprinted with permission.

As you read, consider the following questions:

1. Why would a robot jet fighter have an unprecedented ability to turn, dive, and climb, according to the authors?

2. Why do the authors say it is inevitable that military robots will gain increasing autonomy?

3. According to the authors, why did armies first take up guns?

The annals of warfare are replete with technological innovations that brought lasting change, altering the balance of geopolitical power: the introduction of submarines and machine guns during the U.S. Civil War, aircraft and chemical weapons in World War I, and radar and the atomic bomb in World War II. But the conflicts in Iraq and Afghanistan show evidence of what could well be the most profound change in military history.

For the first time since the earliest antagonists went at each other with sticks and stones, the U.S. military is on the verge of what might be called no-fear warfare—with human combatants replaced by mechanical robots manipulated by people thousands of miles distant. Military robots already are being designed and deployed to perform an array of disagreeable tasks, including forward reconnaissance, stopping and questioning suspicious individuals, and launching artillery. They are being built to navigate rough, hostile terrain, to creep along the ground, patrol waters and skies, and climb up the sides of buildings—all without drawing salaries or objecting to multiple tours of duty.

But what makes military robots profoundly different from human soldiers is that they are incapable of fear—the one battlefield constant since the dawn of history, implicit in the writings of every military theorist since Sun Tzu. Strange though it may sound, within a decade or so, the world's most advanced military could largely eliminate fear as an accompaniment to doing battle—for individual combatants as well as for generals and political leaders charged with deciding how and where to commit their forces.

Absence of Feelings

As in a work of science fiction, a robotic, no-fear military will have no concern for self-preservation; no feelings about the enemy or toward fellow robotic soldiers; no impulse to turn and run; and no motivation other than a set of programmed instructions. An army of robots could be the ideal way to combat fanatical insurgents, including suicide bombers, and it could be a force multiplier against a more conventional enemy. The best-equipped, most physically fit jet pilot, for example, can withstand an acceleration force of about nine Gs— that is, nine times the force of gravity at sea level. With no human aboard, an advanced jet fighter could easily withstand 16 Gs, giving it unprecedented ability to turn, dive and climb.

Robots under development have the potential not just to fire upon an enemy, but also to defuse mines and roadside bombs. Shallow sea beds have long posed a problem for sonar and radar because rocks, reefs and other jagged formations can make it difficult for them to pick out an enemy mine or submarine. For tiny submersible robots crawling along the ocean bottom, such tasks might be routine.

To date, there has been little discussion of the far-reaching cultural and political implications of a robotic military. The advent of robotic warfare cannot help but affect the basic character, structure and practices of the armed forces. Indeed, the U.S. military's very soul could be at stake. What kinds of people might be suited and attracted to military life in this brave new world of no-fear combat? What kind of leadership and training will be needed, and, on a more philosophical level, what's to become of such timeless military values as courage, valor, honor and self-sacrifice? Would these concepts still have meaning in a military in which only the enemy's lives would be at risk?

These are but a few of the questions and concerns that surround the prospect of a robotic military. What will happen when increasingly sophisticated robotic technologies allow the U.S. armed forces to wage war without putting its human soldiers in harm's way? And, most frighteningly, what if some foreign military power backed by superior engineering talent manages to assemble an advanced robotic force before the U.S. does?

The era of no-fear warfare lies just over the horizon. The technology is progressing rapidly, and its appeal is apt to prove irresistible. Within one to two decades, it is likely that our military front line will be dominated by an array of high-tech gizmos, with increasing ability to move and act autonomously. When that happens, on whom will we pin medals—and whom will we hold accountable when something goes wrong?

The U.S. already has deployed a few thousand robots, chiefly UAVs, in Iraq and Afghanistan, and many more ingenious devices are on the way. By 2010, a third of all U.S. deep-strike aircraft likely will be unmanned and, by 2015, Congress insists that a third of U.S. ground combat vehicles be unmanned, as well. When fully developed, these robots will be ideal for what militarists call "3-D work"—tasks that are dirty, dull and dangerous, which describes a great deal of what military forces do. Some robots will be as large as trucks or planes, others as small as dust mites, which may invite troubling comparison with chemical and biological warfare. South Korea already is considering deployment of a fully armed, Samsung-built sentry robot. Because the SGR-A1 robots are unaffected by severe weather and fatigue, Samsung says, "the perfect guarding operation is guaranteed." You can see the SGR-A1 in action on YouTube (http://www.youtube.com). Search for "Samsung robotic sentry."

Will future robots think and act of their own accord as they do in movies such as *Star Wars* and *The Terminator*? At the moment, most military robots are in a first evolutionary phase in which, like puppets, they are under direct human control—although some have semi-autonomous traits. It is almost inevitable, however, that military robots will gain increasing autonomy—first because advances in artificial intelligence will permit it; second, because the sheer number of robots likely to be deployed will challenge the ability of human controllers to remain hands-on; and third, because any network-centric approach to controlling robotic forces eventually could invite enemy hacking.

As with any new technology, it also is predictable that accidents will occur and innocent people will be harmed before the advent of no-fear warfare. When that happens, military and civilian authorities, not to mention tort lawyers, will face the challenging prospect of assigning blame for any deaths or injuries. Such developments will not, of course, be confined to the armed forces. Writing in *Scientific American* in December 2006, no less a seer than Bill Gates predicted that robots were destined to become a "nearly ubiquitous part of our day-to-day lives."

Gates' article compares the present-day state of the robotics industry to that of the personal computer 30 years ago. Indeed, robots offer vast potential for increasing convenience and creating wealth. Few would object to robots taking on dangerous, repetitive tasks, helping the infirm get in and out of bed or even walking the dog on a rainy day. But there's a hitch where the military is concerned, and it's a big one: The introduction of increasingly effective, increasingly autonomous military robots may threaten the values and esprit de corps that always have bound together troops and for which our fighting forces are justly celebrated. Can military culture and the military's basic operating model survive the advent of no-fear warfare? Possibly, but not without substantial changes.

Some early signs of strain already are visible. For example, many of the pilots who control UAVs in Iraq and Afghanistan are stationed in the U.S., where they are safe from harm and routinely go home at night to their families. Nonetheless, some of these desk-bound pilots have claimed to suffer post-traumatic stress disorder as a result of what they've witnessed on their computer monitors; some are even clamoring to receive combat decorations. One veteran who recently returned from Iraq says such claims are stirring active resentment among the "boots on the ground" who must endure daily artillery fire and the risk of attack by improvised explosive devices.

Band of Brothers

At the heart of our basic military model is a set of assumptions known to every general, every drill sergeant and every grunt who survives boot camp. Fanatics and psychopaths aside, few people take naturally to armed conflict. In other circumstances, faced with the terrifying prospect of face-to-face combat, many people would simply turn and run. Armies throughout history have learned to counter this most human of instincts by carefully instilling their troops with a close band-of-brothers camaraderie. Drill sergeants are famously adept at molding recruits into an effective fighting force, not by preaching righteous abstractions at them but by instilling a sense of mission and fostering strong ties of loyalty among fellow troops. By the same token, every good general and every good platoon leader shares the same basic goals upon entering battle: to subdue the enemy forces with minimal loss of their own troops' lives.

With robots replacing people in battle, a fundamental shift in needs and priorities will occur. Rather than technology supporting human combatants, it will be the other way around. The military will need more people with the talent and experience to devise and maintain robotic forces and many fewer—or perhaps none at all—who exhibit the classic traits of a warrior. In other words, the ideal military recruit may come to resemble Bill Gates more than Audie Murphy or Rambo. Or if not Gates, how about a 12-year-old Doritos-munching couch potato who happens to be an ace at playing video games?

In truth, there may be little real difference in the skills required to master a computer game and those required to fly a UAV. Every middle-class parent knows that children born in the computer age far exceed their elders when it comes to electronic gamesmanship. The arrival of military robots, therefore, coincides with a generation of young people whose thumbs and fingers can manipulate the controller of an Xbox or PlayStation with amazing dexterity and confidence.

Moreover, it is often observed that those born in the age of computers, video games and BlackBerries have an unusual facility for multitasking—possibly at the expense of acquiring better face-to-face interpersonal skills and deeper analytical capacity. What could be more adaptive for an age of video-controlled military hardware?

A robotic military model has important implications for recruitment and staffing. When the role of military technology is mainly to support human warriors, it shares many operational characteristics with the industrial manufacturing model: Mass-production of technology allows the military to maintain an effective fighting force despite an ever-changing roster of human combatants. When guns displaced the bow and arrow in the 13th century, for example, it was not because they were more accurate or deadly. Armies first took up guns because they were easier to produce than bows and arrows and because a soldier could be trained to fire one in about half an hour, whereas a good archer might take years to master his weapon.

But consider the nature of a military in which people's primary role is to support the technology, not the other way

Making Killing Easier

But as journalist Chuck Klosterman put it, a person playing video games is usually "not a benevolent God." We do things in the virtual world, daring and violent things, that we would never do if we were there in person. Transferred to war, this could mean that the robotic technologies that make war less intimate and more mediated might well reduce the likelihood of anger-fueled rages, but also make some soldiers too calm, too unaffected by killing. Many studies, like Army psychologist Dave Grossman's seminal book *On Killing* (1995), have shown how disconnecting a person, especially via distance, makes killing easier and abuses and atrocities more likely. D. Keith Shurtleff, an Army chaplain and the ethics instructor for the Soldier Support Institute at Fort Jackson in South Carolina, worries that "as war becomes safer and easier, as soldiers are removed from the horrors of war and see the enemy not as humans but as blips on a screen, there is a very real danger of losing the deterrent that such horrors provide."

P.W. Singer,
"Military Robots and the Laws of War,"
The New Atlantis, *Winter 2009.*
www.thenewatlantis.com.

around. Such a military would demand increasing levels of technical expertise, rendering the idea of a two- or three-year tour of service unthinkable. Once trained, good military roboticists would be much too valuable to let go.

One option might be outsourcing. The military always has relied on the private sector for specialized technology—for designing and building its fighter jets, for example. Because robotic warfare will require intense technological expertise, might we eventually outsource combat operations to companies such as Microsoft, Google or Electronic Arts?

More frightening to contemplate is the possibility that our military's most iconic and enduring figure—the drill sergeant—might become extinct. After all, with human soldiers no longer needing to engage in armed combat, why prepare them for it? Just as muscles tend to atrophy when they go unused, it is conceivable that after a long, successful period of a robotically oriented military, our knowledge of how to organize, train and motivate people for combat could evaporate.

Ethics and Pragmatism

The ethical implications are, of course, profound. The automaton that acquires human consciousness and then turns hostile toward humanity has been a staple of popular entertainment since Czech playwright Karel Capek coined the word robot in his 1921 drama, *R.U.R.* (Rossum's Universal Robots). In 1942, Isaac Asimov, the prolific science-fiction author, introduced three rules that builders of all robots in his stories would have to obey:

1. A robot may not injure a human being or, through inaction, allow a human being to come to harm.

2. A robot must obey orders given it by human beings except where such orders would conflict with the First Law.

3. A robot must protect its own existence as long as such protection does not conflict with the First or Second Law.

As an example of life imitating art, South Korea's Ministry of Commerce, Industry and Energy says it might draw upon Asimov's rules in issuing formal ethics rules for the manufacture of non-military robots, the BBC reported in March 2007.

But rules can be broken. Some roboticists say we are only 10 to 15 years away from having robots that can think and learn like humans. And as robots acquire self-learning mechanisms, said Gianmarco Veruggio of Genoa's Institute of Intelligent Systems for Automation, their behavior will become impossible to fully predict. Noel Sharkey, a professor of artificial intelligence and robotics at the University of Sheffield, asserts that robots' autonomy will make them different than other weapons systems.

"We are going to give decisions on human fatality to machines that are not bright enough to be called stupid," he said.

It is also worth contemplating the effect a no-fear robotic army would likely have upon an enemy. Any human foe faced with the impossibility of confronting and defeating any live soldiers on the field—after all, what glory or satisfaction would there be in killing a robot—might be all the more tempted to adopt terrorist tactics that strike directly at civilians. In the long run, therefore, a no-fear military has the potential to simply transfer fear from the battlefield to society at large.

These considerations notwithstanding, the U.S. military has little choice but to continue its aggressive pursuit of robot technology—because of its potential to spare the lives of U.S. soldiers, because of the enormous advantages that will naturally accrue to the first-mover in robot technology, and because allowing any other military power to get there first would be unacceptable.

And as with the atomic bomb, the introduction of robotic, no-fear warfare is all but certain to spur an intense global arms race. As that happens, the greatest threat to continued U.S. military leadership would come not from insurgent extremists but more likely from any nation with the commitment and discipline to educate and train a superior work force of robotics scientists and engineers.

"Based on the fact that the staff has to deal with huge volume of information in a very short time period DSS [decision support systems] would be helpful in any step of the operation planning process."

Artificial Intelligence Can Improve Military Decision Making

Gabriela Prelipcean, Mircea Boscoianu, and Florin Moisescu

Gabriela Prelipcean is a professor at the University of Suceava in Romania; Mircea Boscoianu and Florin Moisescu are professors at the Air Force Academy in Brasov, Romania. In the following viewpoint, they argue that military decision making is very complex and may overwhelm human planners. They suggest that artificial intelligence (AI) computer systems can help human military planners determine a course of action. The authors conclude

Gabriela Prelipcean, Mircea Boscoianu, and Florin Moisescu, "New Ideas on the Artificial Intelligence Support in Military Applications," World Scientific and Engineering Academy and Society, 2010, pp. 34, 37. Reprinted with permission. **Conference Title:** 9th WSEAS Int. Conf. on ARTIFICIAL INTELLIGENCE, KNOWLEDGE ENGINEERING AND DATA BASES (AIKED '10); **Proceedings Title:** "RECENT ADVANCES IN ARTIFICIAL INTELLIGENCE, KNOWLEDGE ENGINEERING AND DATA BASES"; **Location:** University of Cambridge, UK, February 20–22, 2010; **ISBN:** 978-960-474-154-0; **pp.** 34-39; **Paper's Link:** http://www.wseas.us/e-library/conferences/2010/Cambridge/AIKED/AIKED-04.pdf; **Conference Page:** http://www.wseas.us/conferences/2010/cambridge/aiked/; **Publisher:** WSEAS (www.wseas.org).

that AI can allow the analysis of more military options, as well as provide a deeper analysis of those options.

As you read, consider the following questions:

1. Why do the authors say human capability in analyzing military data is insufficient on the modern battlefield?

2. What are the six steps in the military planning process, according to the authors?

3. According to the authors, why could wargaming be a frustrating tool for the military?

M ilitary decision making demands an increasing ability to understand and structure the critical information on the battlefield. As the military evolves into a networked force, decision makers should select and filter information across the battlefield in a timely and efficient manner. Human capability in analyzing all the data is not sufficient because the modern battlefield is characterized by dramatic movements, unexpected evolutions, chaotic behavior and non-linear situations. The Artificial Intelligence (AI) ingredient permits [decision makers] to explore a greater range of options, enabling the staff to analyze more possible options in the same amount of time, together with a deeper analysis of these options.

AI Can Help

Military decision [makers] should consider information about a huge range of assets and capabilities (human resources, combat and support vehicles, helicopters, sophisticated intelligence and communication equipment, artillery and missiles) that may perform complex tasks of multiple types: collection of intelligence, movements, direct/indirect fires, infrastructure, and transports.

The decisional factor needs an integrated framework capable to perform the critical steps, from capturing a high-level course of action (CoA) to realizing a detailed analysis/plan of tasks and one possibility is to be based on different AI techniques, ranging from qualitative spatial interpretation of CoA diagrams to interleaved adversarial scheduling.

Given the logistics consumption and the complexity of time/space analysis, the classic decisional process is time and manpower consuming and is dramatically limiting the number and diversity of options able to explore and analyze.

The military planning process is typically composed on the following steps: *initiation*: corresponds to mission trigger and task reception; *orientation*: includes mission assessment, mission statement and decision maker's planning guidance; *concept development*: includes staff's analysis, friendly and enemy courses of action development and analysis, and decision maker's estimate; *decision*: includes courses of action comparison and selection, course of action approval, decision maker's direction, review of critical assumptions; *plan development*: mainly concerned by synchronization and finalization; *plan review*: includes analysis and revision of plans.

Elaboration, mitigation and evaluation of different CoAs are significant steps in planning process. CoA development and analysis are exercises in which are simulated different situations. Time constrains the process to generate a complete range of CoAs, and evaluate them according to significant point of views, before selecting and executing the optimal one. . . .

Volume of Information

CoA design is based on the understanding of the situation assessment, mission analysis, resources status assessment. According on the time available, the decision staff should develop different CoAs that answer to some critical questions (when, who, what, where, why and how), each of them suitable, feasible, acceptable, exclusive, complete. The analysis of these CoAs could be based on war gaming simulations even if some authors considered that war gaming could be a frustrating tool for the military since the selected CoA is never war-gamed sufficiently to achieve synchronization. Based on the fact that the staff has to deal with huge volume of information in a very short time period DSS [decision support systems—that is AI computer programs] would be helpful in any step of the operation planning process.

DSS-CoA should be based on a detailed investigation of how the staff perform CoAs evaluation, analysis, selection. Since the evaluations of the CoAs according to the different criteria might include uncertainty, ambiguity, fuzziness, subjectivity is necessary to minimize the risk component introduced during the evaluation process. A graphical and intuitive tool could balance the relative importance of the set of criteria.

> "Driverless highways and vehicles could
> produce tremendous benefits, at least
> equal to the benefits generated by the
> original interstate highway system."

AI Smart Cars Will Transform Highway Safety and Congestion

Randal O'Toole

Randal O'Toole is a Cato Institute senior fellow working on urban growth and transporation issues. In the following viewpoint, he argues that the technology for driverless cars is currently available. Implementing that technology would, he says, reduce congestion and increase safety. He concludes that objections to driverless cars have no merit. The question, he says, is not whether to move toward driverless cars, but rather which of several adoption scenarios would be the best.

As you read, consider the following questions:

1. How many vehicles does O'Toole say can be moved on modern freeway lanes at 60 mph, and how many cars does he say could be moved in driverless lanes at the same speed?

Randal O'Toole, "Dude, Where's My Driverless Car?" *Gridlock: Why We're Stuck in Traffic and What To Do About It*, Cato Institute, 2009, pp. 189–202. Reprinted with permission.

2. What did *USA Today* list as one of the twenty-five most important inventions of the past twenty-five years?

3. What does O'Toole say are the disadvantages of the do-nothing model of introducing driverless cars?

D riverless highways and vehicles could produce tremendous benefits, at least equal to the benefits generated by the original interstate highway system. First, moving from human-controlled to electronically controlled vehicles would nearly quadruple the capacity of existing roads to move traffic. At 60 miles per hour, modern freeway lanes can move no more than 2,200 vehicles per hour. By safely reducing the distances between vehicles, driverless lanes could move at least 8,000 vehicles per hour at the same speed. In most urban areas, this would nearly eliminate the need for new highway construction for several decades.

Faster Reactions, Fewer Errors

Second, because computer reaction times are so much faster than a human's, driverless highways would eliminate the kind of congestion that results when one car in a line briefly slows down. A highway lane capable of moving 2,200 vehicles per hour at 60 miles per hour might be capable of moving only 1,600 vehicles per hour at 30 miles per hour. If that highway lane is loaded with, say, 1,800 vehicles per hour and one car slows down to 30, however briefly, traffic will remain at 30 miles per hour—or less—until flows fall below 1,600 vehicles per hour. This is why people often find themselves stuck in congestion that has no visible cause.

Third, by virtually eliminating driver error, which causes a majority of fatal highway accidents, these systems would greatly increase highway safety. Reducing accidents would not only save lives, it would save the time of people who would otherwise be stuck in congestion caused by accidents.

By reducing congestion, driverless cars would increase average urban speeds, giving people access to more resources. By offering more precise driving, driverless cars would make possible higher top speeds on existing roads. Though few of today's roads may be suitable for [artist and highway visionary Norman] Bel Geddes' 100 miles per hour, speeds in many areas could be raised above today's typical limits of 65 to 75 miles per hour.

Driverless systems would save energy by eliminating stop-and-go congestion. In the long run, driverless cars would reach higher speeds without increasing fuel consumption. Today's automobiles are designed to allow occupants to survive in the event of a variety of accidents. But driverless cars would likely reduce most kinds of accidents, allowing manufacturers to build lighter-weight cars that would still be safer and far more fuel-efficient [than] today's cars.

While no system is perfect, an electronic system is much less prone to error than one relying on humans. People whose desktop computers suffer frequent system crashes may find this hard to believe, but the truth is that automobiles are already loaded with scores of microprocessors controlling fuel injection, automatic transmissions, cruise control, anti-lock brakes, airbags, climate control, instrument panels, and literally thousands of other functions. These microprocessors are controlled by up to 100 million lines of software code—close to 15 times as many lines as are used to operate Boeing's latest 787 aircraft. Automobile owners will soon be able to install software upgrades simply by plugging their car into a computer communications port. Making cars driverless would, in many cases, require little more than the installation of one or two sensors and another piece of software.

Driverless Vehicles Today

Bel Geddes predicted Americans would travel in driverless vehicles by 1960. Yet, 50 years later, driverless vehicles still seem like something out of science fiction. In fact, . . . advances in highway and driving technologies seem to have ended some time in the 1950s.

To be fair, some advances have been made in roadway and auto technology since the 1950s, but most have been oriented to safety, fuel economy, and power rather than to speed and traffic flows. Of the latter kinds of advances, most are not yet widespread enough to significantly improve traffic flows and speeds.

One of these advances, electronic tolling, is significant enough that *USA Today* listed it as one of the 25 most important inventions of the past 25 years. . . . Electronic tolling not only eliminates delays at the tollbooths, it eases the use of congestion pricing, in which tolls are adjusted to rise enough that roads never become congested. Although more than a dozen states use electronic tolling, congestion pricing has so far been implemented on only a dozen or so highways in nine states, plus a number of bridges and tunnels, mostly in the New York City area.

Other advances have been made to automobiles and involve the use of radar or lasers to detect other vehicles around the car. Adaptive cruise control detects if a vehicle is in front of the car and automatically adjusts speed, using either the accelerator or brakes, to maintain a safe distance behind that vehicle. All the driver has to do is set a top speed and steer. Adaptive cruise control not only increases highway safety, it reduces the kind of congestion caused by slow human reflexes. Traffic engineers at the University of Minnesota estimate that congestion will significantly decline when as few as 20 percent of cars on the road are using adaptive cruise control—which is expected by 2010.

Supplementing adaptive cruise control, Nissan, Honda, and Toyota are now selling cars with "lane keep assist systems" that steer themselves on highways. A camera detects lane stripes, and the car stays between the stripes. Legally, drivers must keep their hands on the wheel, but the car will resist efforts to deviate from the lanes without signaling a lane change. Such cars have been available in Japan since at least 2001, in Europe since 2004, and will begin to enter the United States in 2010.

New cars are also being made with collision avoidance systems that use radar or lasers to detect vehicles behind or in drivers' blind spots. Volkswagen, Raytheon, and other companies have taken these systems the next step by developing cars that can safely change lanes in traffic, for example, to overtake slow-moving vehicles.

Some other intermediate technologies are on the horizon. One is the idea of intelligent intersections that wirelessly communicate with motor vehicles. Such an intersection might warn on-coming vehicles that vehicles will be crossing their path or that a light is about to turn red or green. The Institute of Electrical and Electronics Engineers has drafted a communications standard for wireless communications among vehicles and between vehicles and traffic control devices. The combination of all these technologies—adaptive cruise control, collision avoidance, lane keep assistance, and wireless communications between intersections and vehicles—effectively enables driverless cars on major highways. . . .

Four Scenarios for Driverless Vehicle Adoption

The American automobile fleet turns over about every 18 years. This means that, once perfected, driverless vehicles could become dominant within a decade and universal soon after that. Most of the people reading this [viewpoint] are likely to see widespread adoption of driverless vehicles in their lifetimes. But this advance can be hastened or slowed by government action or restraint. Here are four ways in which the chicken-and-egg problem and other obstacles to driverless vehicles might be overcome.

The Do-Nothing Model. Driverless vehicles will eventually be introduced even if no government policy actively promotes them. Early models will initially operate on private roads. For example, many private forestland owners manage their own road systems and might introduce driverless vehicles on those roads to transport timber from forest to mill. Similarly, driverless passenger services might start on private systems such as golf courses and freight yards.

Shipping companies might propose that states allow convoys of trucks, with the first truck operated by a driver followed by one or more driverless trucks which are programmed to follow the first one. Driverless buses may initially work on routine journeys such as between air terminals and parking lots. Eventually, states will legalize driverless cars on highways or city streets. The disadvantage of the do-nothing model is that it may take an extra decade or more before the full benefits of driverless vehicles can be realized.

The Computer Model. Whether you are the proud owner of a Mac, a Dell, or any other brand of personal computer, most of the components in the sleek outer casing of your machine are identical to or closely resemble off-the-shelf products that anyone with a little expertise could buy and assemble into a functional computer (though it would probably cost far more than to simply buy a ready-made machine). Nearly all of the parts inside a typical laptop, including the processor, graphics chip, memory chips, disk drives, screen, and keyboard, communicate with one another using hardware and software standards developed by the computer industry.

A consortium including Intel, Compaq, Microsoft, Digital, IBM, and Northern Telecom originally developed the standard USB port now available on most computers. A consortium including Apple, Texas Instruments, Sony, IBM, DEC, and Thomson originally designed the somewhat competing Firewire port. Similar standards govern communications between hard drives and other devices inside the computers. Regardless of who originally creates the standards, they are openly published with the hope and expectation that a wide variety of manufacturers will make products that use them. . . .

Successful adoption of driverless vehicles will clearly require the development of industry standards. Several questions will have to be answered: Should driverless vehicles . . . [incorporate] some sort of driverless features into highways, or . . . [should they build] all driverless capabilities into the vehicles themselves? Should driverless vehicles operate on the same roads as driver-operated vehicles, or should some roads be set aside for driverless operations and others for driver-operated vehicles? What kind of communications should take place among vehicles and between vehicles and highway features such as intersections? Who is liable if a driverless vehicle gets into an accident: the owner or the manufacturer?

Government Involvement

The HDTV Model. The short story behind high-definition television (HDTV) [a kind of television with a high-quality picture] is that the Federal Communications Commission [FCC] encouraged television manufacturers to develop a new standard and then smoothed the way for that standard to be put in place on a rigorous timetable. This model could be adapted to highways by having the Department of Transportation play the role of the FCC in promoting driverless standards and then mandating that those standards be applied to some or all highways by a certain date.

The long story behind HDTV makes this model a lot less appealing. Unlike rapidly changing computer technology, changes in television technologies have been slow, and the political nature of the FCC is largely responsible. For example, CBS began broadcasting in color in 1950. Yet it took 17 more years before all three major networks broadcast most of their programming in color. Much of that delay was caused by FCC

"What with smart cars and cell phones, we have created mobile telephone booths."

dithering and political maneuvering by the major networks trying to get an advantage over their competitors.

The same thing happened with HDTV. The FCC initiated efforts to introduce HDTV in 1987, and the basic digital

HDTV standard was developed by 1994. But this was followed by years of political debate and lobbying over the best use of the extremely valuable portions of the radio spectrum that the FCC allocated to television broadcasters. At certain points in this debate, it appeared that HDTV would never be implemented. One of the FCC's early targets was to have HDTV completely replace conventional broadcasting by May 1, 2002. They missed this target by seven years, which in the computer industry would be several generations of new products.

Still, the European Commission seems to be following the HDTV model. It launched an intelligent car initiative in 2006 aimed at removing the barriers to implementing intelligent vehicles. This initiative aims to build a consensus among the key players involved, remove the legal and institutional barriers, and stimulate consumer demand for the new technologies. Among other things, the program has dedicated a radio frequency for road safety and traffic management.

The Cell Phone Model. The cell phone model is a hybrid. Like the computer industry, cell phone technology changes rapidly as users purchase successively powerful new phones capable of texting, photography, video, and internet communications. Competition is the driving force behind advances in cell phone technology, with at least five major networks (AT&T, Nextel, T-Mobile, US Cellular, and Verizon) supplemented by many local providers. Like television broadcasting, however, cell phones use a share of the radio spectrum, keeping the hand of government in the mix. Still, thus far, the cell phone model seems superior to the glacial pace of technological change in the television industry. . . .

Objections to Driverless Cars

The main opposition to driverless vehicles is likely to come from the same anti-mobility coalition that opposes today's automobiles. Even if driverless cars were powered by renewable, nonpolluting sources of energy, many would still object to them because of their contributions to sprawl.

Driverless highways can potentially carry four times as much traffic as driver-operated roads. Yet opponents will claim that this extra capacity would quickly be filled up by people who were induced to drive more. . . . So-called "induced demand" is more accurately described as "suppressed demand." As long as people pay the costs, anything that increases mobility should be regarded as good, not bad.

No doubt driverless vehicles will contribute to the further decentralization of urban areas, that is, "sprawl." The question is, What's wrong with that? The opponents of decentralization claim that Americans were forced to sprawl by misguided government policies such as Federal Housing Administration "redlining" of inner-city neighborhoods, or that they were encouraged to sprawl by government subsidies to roads and other infrastructure. The solution in either case is to fix the policies, not to prohibit sprawl through heavy-handed land-use regulation and anti-mobility plans.

Driverless vehicles and driverless highways represent the next mobility revolution. Like previous revolutions, from the steamboat and canal to the automobile, the driverless revolution is likely to produce massive economic, social, and personal benefits. Moreover, as with the automobile, but unlike previous revolutions such as the railroad those benefits are likely to be shared by nearly everyone in America. The question is not whether to promote driverless vehicles but what policies will lead to the most rapid and widespread adaptation of driverless technologies.

> "This phenomenon, where improved safety spurs on greater risk taking, is known as risk compensation."

AI Smart Cars Will Have Only a Limited Effect on Safety

Steve G. Steinberg

Steve G. Steinberg is a technology consultant who has written for Wired *and the* Los Angeles Times. *In the following viewpoint, he argues that one of the most interesting advances in artificial intelligence (AI) in the near future will involve driverless cars. He says that the impetus for driverless cars is the fact that automobile fatalities have ceased to drop since the 1990s. However, he argues, though smart cars are safer, the fact that they are safer will cause some drivers to drive more recklessly. As a result, smart cars will not reduce fatalities as much as their proponents hope.*

As you read, consider the following questions:

1. What is the Maes-Garreau horizon, according to the viewpoint?

2. Why does Steinberg say that people who think electric cars are revolutionary are delusional?

Steve G. Steinberg, "New Developments in AI," http://blog.steinberg.org, July 3, 2010. Reprinted with permission.

3. According to Steinberg, what experiment did British researchers use to prove that risk compensation exists?

Thanks to popular culture, we have a good idea of what to expect when "strong" AI [artificial intelligence, that is machines with human-like intelligence] arrives. Machines attain consciousness? Prepare to be harvested as food. Detroit introduces talking cars? *"Hello, Kit".*[1]

Weak AI

What to expect in the near-term is less clear. While strong AI still lies safely beyond the Maes-Garreau horizon (a vanishing point, perpetually fifty years ahead) a host of important new developments in weak AI [machines with intelligence but not consciousness] are poised to be commercialized in the next few years. But because these developments are a paradoxical mix of intelligence and stupidity, they defy simple forecasts, they resist hype. They are not unambiguously better, cheaper, or faster. They are something new.

What are the implications of a car that adjusts its speed to avoid collisions ... but occasionally mistakes the guardrail along a sharp curve as an oncoming obstacle and slams on the brakes? What will it mean when our computers know everything—every single fact, the entirety of human knowledge—but can only reason at the level of a cockroach?

I mention these specific examples—smart cars and massive knowledge-bases—because they came up repeatedly in my recent conversations with AI researchers. These experts expressed little doubt that both technologies will reach the market far sooner, and penetrate it more pervasively, than most people realize.

But confidence to the point of arrogance is practically a degree requirement for computer scientists. Which, actually, is another reason why these particular developments caught my

1. In the 1980s television series *Knight Rider*, there was an AI car named Kit.

interest: for all their confidence about the technologies *per se*, every researcher I spoke to admitted they had no clue—but were intensely curious—how these developments will affect society.

Taking that as a signal these technologies are worth understanding I started to do some digging. While I am still a long way from any answers, I think I've honed in on some of the critical questions.

Autonomous Automobiles

There is a sense of excitement that infects everyone, whether Detroit exec or Silicon Valley VC [venture capitalist], who is involved with electric cars. It comes from the belief, propagated by an enthralled media, that what they are doing is important—even vital. Electric vehicles, they insist, are revolutionary.

They are delusional.

Whether a car runs on gas, electricity, or steam, it remains a deadly weapon, with victims denominated not just in bodies, but in wasted wages and lost time. No matter what your attitude toward suburbs and urban sprawl (personally, I'm a fan) anyone who has tried driving the I405 at rush hour knows that cars need far more than a new motor.

But, fortuitously, the hype over the electrical car is providing covering fire for a true revolution: the *computational* car. It is the increasingly autonomous intelligence of automobiles, far more than a new drive train, that stands to fundamentally alter how we interact with cars, and how they affect our planet.

Already, more than a dozen 2010 car-year models offer intelligent safety features such as lane departure warning and adaptive cruise control. Crucially, they do not just flash a light or sound a buzzer when a problem is detected: they *autonomously* apply the brakes or adjust the steering. The driver is no longer the fail-safe that ensures the machine is running correctly. The driver is a problem to work around. The driver, you might say, is a bug.

Of course, I am far from the first to recognize the importance of this development. Even *Wards*, the automotive trade weekly, recently acknowledged that artificial intelligence is poised to change cars more thoroughly than electric propulsion ever will. And Brad Templeton, a well-known 'net entrepreneur, has written extensively and persuasively on how today's intelligent safety features will inexorably lead to autonomous vehicles.

Making this technology all the more notable is that it wasn't supposed to happen.

For many years, the conventional wisdom, certainly within the auto industry, was that carmakers would never introduce intelligent safety features so long as there were plaintiff lawyers. Autonomous technology shifted the liability for accidents from the car's owner to the car's maker, said industry spokespeople, and was tantamount to corporate suicide.

Three developments changed their minds. First, active safety technologies have become substantially more robust, thanks to improvements in sensor design, and, most importantly, in sensor fusion and planning algorithms. Second, drive-by-wire has rendered the legal debate largely academic— car functions are already mediated by computers, one way or another. Lastly, and probably most importantly, the auto industry experienced an unprecedented, violently destabilizing, massive contraction. Technology that previously seemed like a grave, existential threat now seems like the least of their problems. It turns out that, innovation, like freedom, "is just another word for having nothing left to lose."

Automobile Fatalities

All those developments made autonomous technology possible, even practical. But the impetus to actually *do* something

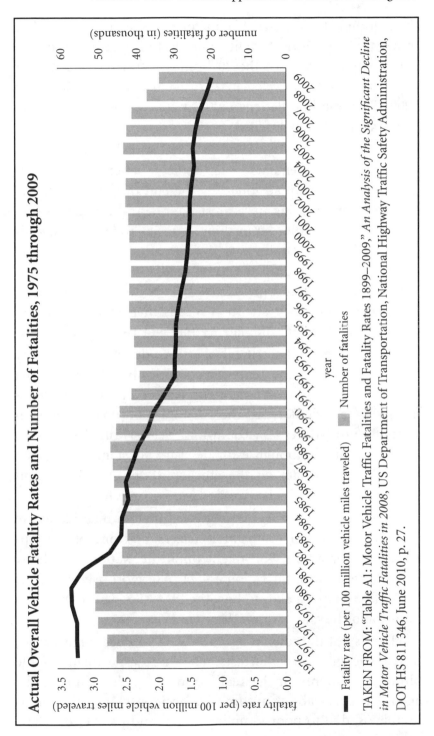

Actual Overall Vehicle Fatality Rates and Number of Fatalities, 1975 through 2009

fatality rate (per 100 million vehicle miles traveled)

number of fatalities (in thousands)

year

▬ Fatality rate (per 100 million vehicle miles traveled)   ▉ Number of fatalities

TAKEN FROM: "Table A1: Motor Vehicle Traffic Fatalities and Fatality Rates 1899–2009," *An Analysis of the Significant Decline in Motor Vehicle Traffic Fatalities in 2008*, US Department of Transportation, National Highway Traffic Safety Administration, DOT HS 811 346, June 2010, p. 27.

about it came from charts like the one [in the insert]. The line shows the automotive fatality rate declining steadily for the last twenty-five years of the 20th century, from 3.5 deaths per 100 million miles traveled in 1975 to just over 1.5 deaths in 2000. Then the line flattens out. For the last ten years the fatality rate has barely budged.

The gains in the 1980s and 1990s stemmed primarily from mechanical improvements in car bodies—better vertical rigidity, intentional crumple zones. By the end of the millennium, engineers were butting up against the physical limits of materials, chasing rapidly diminishing returns. Today, any significant decline in the fatality rate will have to come from changes in how cars are driven—or, ideally, *not* driven. And pressure is mounting: the extraordinary growth in texting and its deleterious effects on driver attention means that even holding everything else constant, the fatality rate will rise.

This still begs the critical question: do intelligent safety features *work?* Do they save lives and limbs? We know that changing lanes unintentionally and rear-ending a forward vehicle—the accident types the two most popular intelligent safety features address—account for a very significant percentage of fatalities, although estimates vary substantially. But we have almost no data on the efficacy of the new intelligent safety solutions, and what we do have is contested.

This uncertainty is surprising given that auto accidents are the leading cause of death for teenagers, and one of the top-ten causes for adults. You might think the National Highway Traffic Safety Administration [NHTSA] rigorously evaluates new safety features, akin to how the FDA [Food and Drug Administration] evaluates new drugs and devices.

That is not the case. At best, the NHTSA does some simple, unrealistic *in vitro* style tests. They never perform double blind experiments in the real world. Even the statistics the agency collects about automotive accidents are of dubious usefulness, due to poor sampling design and paucity of detail.

Still, we can thank the NHTSA for a recent report that at least throws the uncertainty about autonomous safety features into stark relief. The NHTSA had volunteers drive a test track in cars with automatic lane departure correction, and then interviewed the drivers for their impressions. Although the report does not describe the undoubted look of horror on the examiner's face while interviewing one female, 20-something subject, it does relay the gist of her comments.

After she praised the ability of the car to self-correct when she drifted from her lane, she noted that she would love to have this feature in her own car. Then, after a night of drinking in the city, she would not have to sleep at a friend's house before returning to her rural home.

Risk Compensation

This phenomenon, where improved safety spurs on greater risk taking, is known as risk compensation, or "risk homeostasis". Most of us became familiar with the concept from debates over anti-lock brakes (ABS), but its specter has plagued nearly every attempt to improve automotive safety, from seat belts to night vision. Yet almost nothing about risk compensation—its etiology, its prevalence, its significance—is certain.

To prove the phenomenon even exists, one particularly inspired British researcher had volunteers ride bicycles on a closed course, with half the people wearing helmets and proper attire, and the other half clad in their underwear. Graduate students positioned on the sidelines graded the volunteers performance and tallied any unsafe maneuvers. The results showed that the unclothed group practiced much safer driving habits, thereby supporting risk compensation theory—and Britain's reputation for eccentricity.

Many other, more targeted studies from the 1990s also painted automotive safety as a zero-sum game, with any gains in safety vitiated by greater risk taking. Not only did careful, well-designed experiments in Europe show that anti-lock brakes lead to more aggressive driving, but many of the countries that adopted seat-belt legislation found that auto fatalities barely budged, while the number of pedestrians injured by cars actually increased.

These studies make for fascinating reading but can be hard to integrate with common sense. Anyone who has driven a vintage car *knows* they do not feel as safe. Fortunately, over the last ten years the scholarly consensus has shifted—pushed by both empirical and theoretical developments—to a much more nuanced view. . . .

What they have found is satisfying in its lack of surprise. Concisely, risk compensation exists, but not universally—it is personality dependent. "Sensation seeking" is one blunt-edged, but not totally wrong, way to characterize the people who *do* exhibit risk compensation.

Nonetheless, the insight that intelligent safety features will only help a subset of the population can seem deflating. The big stories in technology are always the ones that surpass expectations.

> *"Because a high fun factor is what sells, the video-game industry has become increasingly keen to make use of developments in AI research—and computer scientists have taken notice."*

AI Research and Video Games Benefit One Another

Jonathan Schaeffer, Vadim Bulitko, and Michael Buro

Jonathan Schaeffer, Vadim Bulitko, and Michael Buro are members of the GAMES group at the University of Alberta, in Canada. In the following viewpoint, they argue that the need for better artificial intelligence (AI) in video games has led game designers to turn to university researchers for help. The authors note that, for example, research advances in pathfinding have made their way into video games. The authors conclude that this kind of collaboration will both improve video games and spur useful advances in AI.

As you read, consider the following questions:

1. How do the authors explain the need for bots to get smarter in terms of badminton?

2. What game do the authors suggest may be joining the ranks of chess and checkers, and why?

3. The authors note that a computer algorithm to calculate the best path between two points is available. What is the problem with using this algorithm in video games?

Y ou're following a gloomy corridor into a large boiler room, dimly lit by a flickering fluorescent lamp and echoing with the rhythms of unseen machinery. Three enemy soldiers suddenly appear on a catwalk high above the floor. They split up, one of them laying down suppressive fire, which forces you to take cover. Although you shoot back, the attackers still manage to creep forward behind a curtain of smoke and flying debris.

Moments later, a machine gun rings out, and you are cut down in a shower of bullets. Then, as you lie dying, you glimpse the soldier who flanked you from behind while his two buddies drew your attention.

Thankfully, it was only a video game, so in fact you're not mortally wounded. Still, your ego might well be bruised, because you were not only outgunned but also outsmarted by artificial intelligence (AI).

The game is called *F.E.A.R.*, short for First Encounter Assault Recon, and its use of AI, along with its impressive graphics, are its prime attractions. The developer, Monolith Productions of Kirkland, Wash., released it in 2005 to rave reviews, including the GameSpot Web site's Best Artificial Intelligence award. Such recognition means a lot to the game's creators, who face stiff competition in what has become a multibillion-dollar industry.

The game is a far cry from the traditional diversions that AI researchers like ourselves have long studied, such as chess and checkers. Whereas the goal in the past was to write computer programs capable of beating expert players at such board games, now the metric of success for AI is whether it makes video games more entertaining.

Because a high fun factor is what sells, the video-game industry has become increasingly keen to make use of developments in AI research—and computer scientists have taken notice. A watershed came in 2000, when John E. Laird, a professor of engineering at the University of Michigan, and Michael van Lent, now chief scientist at Soar Technology, in Ann Arbor, Mich., published a call to arms that described commercial video games as "AI's killer application." Their point was that research to improve AI for such games would create spin-offs in many other spheres.

The main challenge is to make computer-generated characters—dubbed bots—act realistically. They must, of course, look good and move naturally. But, ideally, they should also be able to engage in believable conversations, plan their actions, find their way around virtual worlds, and learn from their mistakes. That is, they need to be smart.

Today many video games create only an illusion of intelligence, using a few programming tricks. But in the not-so-distant future, game bots will routinely use sophisticated AI techniques to shape their behavior. We and our colleagues in the University of Alberta GAMES (Game-playing, Analytical methods, Minimax search and Empirical Studies) research group, in Edmonton, Canada, have been working to help bring about such a revolution.

The AI of *F.E.A.R.* is based loosely on an automated planner called STRIPS (for STanford Research Institute Problem Solver), which Richard E. Fikes and Nils J. Nilsson, both now of Stanford University, developed way back in 1971. The general idea of STRIPS was to establish one or more goals along with a set of possible actions, each of which could be carried out only when its particular preconditions were satisfied. The planning system kept track of the physical environment and determined which actions were allowed. Carrying out one of them in turn modified the state of the environment, which therefore made other actions possible.

The designers of *F.E.A.R.* gave its soldiers such goals as patrolling, killing the player's character, and taking cover to protect their own virtual lives. The makers of the game also gave each kind of bot a set of possible actions with which to accomplish each of its goals. One advantage of this approach is that it saves the developers the burden of trying to specify a response to every situation that might arise. Further, it allows seemingly intelligent behaviors to appear almost magically— such as the maneuver described above.

In that instance, the three attackers were carrying out two types of basic actions. One is to move to covered positions that are as close as possible to the player's character. The other is simply to move around obstacles. The combination creates something that was not explicitly programmed into the game at all: a devastating flanking maneuver.

The spontaneous emergence of such complex behaviors is important because it provides a sense of deeper intelligence. That's really what gets your heart pounding when you play the game. But you'd also like your adversaries to become more cunning over time, and *F.E.A.R.* has no mechanism for accomplishing that.

Why do bots need to get smarter? Imagine a game of badminton in which your opponent always reacts to your serves in the same way, always falls for your drops, and never attempts to anticipate your smashes. It would be a boring match. Up until recently, AI had been able to offer video gamers no better: the imps of *Doom*, released in 1993, never shoot their fireballs preemptively, and the civil-protection officers in *Half-Life 2* (2004) always take the nearest cover while reloading their weapons—to mention just a couple of things players experience with two well-known releases.

The standard solution is to add an element of randomness to the code that controls a bot's decision making. Doing so varies a player's experience, but the result does not necessarily come across as being intelligent.

A better approach is for the computer to learn about the player and to adapt a bot's tactics and strategy appropriately. Of course, you don't want the bot to become so good that it will win all the time; you just want it to give the human player a good run for the money. This capability, known as machine learning, is found in very few commercial games: *Creatures*, from the now-defunct Creature Labs, employed machine learning as early as 1997, as did *Black & White*, developed by the UK-based Lionhead Studios a few years later. But most video games are not able to "learn" on the fly or otherwise adapt to the person playing. Our group is hoping to push things forward in this regard using a system we've created for research purposes called PaSSAGE, which stands for Player-Specific Stories via Automatically Generated Events.

PaSSAGE, as its name implies, is all about storytelling, which has long been a staple of various role-playing games. But video games of all types rely to some extent on engaging storytelling. You can categorize such games by the way they vary their repertoire to appeal to different people.

Some games—*Half-Life* (2001), for example—are immensely popular even though they feature just a single linear story. So good scriptwriting can clearly go a long way. Other games, such as *Star Wars: Knights of the Old Republic* (2003), offer several alternatives to the main plot. This gives you the impression that you can shape your virtual fate—what psychologists call a sense of agency. That feeling of being in control is usually limited, however, because the branching plot lines often merge later on.

Titles like *The Elder Scrolls IV: Oblivion* (2006) and *S.T.A.L.K.E.R.: Shadow of Chernobyl* (2007) work similarly, taking one main story and complementing it with episodes drawn from a library of side quests. Other games, such as *The Sims 2* (2005), go a step further by dispensing with a scripted plot altogether and creating an open-ended world in which players can effectively design their own happenings.

Although each of these techniques has enjoyed success, they all force the designer to make a trade-off between scriptwriter expressiveness and player agency. The approach we've taken with PaSSAGE avoids that conundrum by having the computer learn players' interests and preferences and mold the story to suit them as the game progresses.

PaSSAGE uses the same game engine as *Neverwinter Nights*, a fantasy adventure set in medieval times, produced by BioWare of Edmonton. With PaSSAGE, scriptwriters determine only the most general arc to the story and provide a library of possible encounters the player's character may have. The computer studies the player as he or she progresses and cues in the kinds of experiences that are most desired. For instance, if you like fighting, the game will provide ample opportunities for combat. If you prefer to amass riches, the game will conjure up ways for you to be rewarded for your actions. The software is able to make the sequence of events globally consistent by maintaining a history of the virtual world's changing state and modifying the player's future encounters appropriately. The game will therefore always appear to make sense, even though it unfolds quite differently for different people—or even for the same person as his moods and tastes change.

Machine learning can also be used to formulate the tactics that bots use, a job that now must be handcrafted by a game's designers. Pieter Spronck and his colleagues, of the University

Poker and AI

Poker is currently the world's most played card game. Hundreds of thousands of people play poker every day, and can play in a real life environment or over the internet using a distributed application running a simulation of the game.

One of the biggest reasons for poker's recent success is its fundamental dynamics. The 'hidden' elements of the game means players must observe their opponent's characteristics to be able to arrive at good decisions, given their options. A very good poker player will consistently dominate a sub-optimal opponent, although stochastic elements apply heavy statistical variation to the game, allowing weak players to win occasionally.

The game of poker offers a well-defined domain in which to investigate some fundamental issues in computing science, such as how to handle deliberate misinformation, and how to make intelligent guesses based on partial knowledge.

Patrick McCurley,
"An Artificial Intelligence Agent for Texas Hold 'Em Poker,"
Pokerai.org, 2009. http://pokerai.org/.

of Tilburg, in the Netherlands, demonstrated this ability in 2005 using *Neverwinter Nights*. Spronck had one computer play against computerized opponents, programming it to get better over time by choosing the combat tactics that most often led to victory.

Members of our research group have been following through on Spronck's work with *Neverwinter Nights*, using a different learning algorithm. Other colleagues of ours at the University of Alberta aim to do something similar with a multiplayer online game called *Counter-Strike* (2003), which pits a group of terrorists against a squad of antiterrorist commandos. Each character can be controlled either by a person or by the computer. As with *F.E.A.R.*, players view the virtual world from the perspective of the characters they manipulate, making *Counter-Strike* an example of what's known as a first-person-shooter game.

This project has so far produced a formal system for analyzing and classifying a team's opening moves. That may not sound like much, but this task proved immensely challenging, because positions and actions are not nearly as constrained as they are in a game like chess. Researchers in our group have used this formalism to analyze computer logs of more than 50 hours of tournament-level play between seasoned *Counter-Strike* teams. Soon, we expect, computer bots programmed to learn tactics from such logs will play reasonably well—doing things a person might do. It'll be a long time before these bots will be able to beat expert human players, though. But that's not the objective, after all—they just need to make for entertaining adversaries.

Jeff Orkin and Deb Roy of MIT are undertaking a similar effort with something they call *The Restaurant Game*, for which they are applying machine learning to the task of making bots speak and act believably in social settings. In this case, the bots' behaviors are based on observations gleaned from more than 10,000 sessions of human play.

Machine learning can also pay off for poker, which has become an especially hot game in recent years with the explosion of opportunities for playing it online. The strongest programs for two-player fixed-bet-size poker attempt to calculate the mathematically optimal solution for winning each hand. It turns out that finding such solutions is computationally infeasible, at least right now—there are just too many possible combinations of cards and betting sequences. But members of our research group have devised ways to calculate near-optimal strategies using certain simplifying assumptions. For example, instead of allowing four rounds of betting—which is permitted in competition poker—the program sets the limit at three. By further reducing the complexity of the game in clever ways, the computational burden can be reduced to a reasonable level. BioTools, a commercial spin-off of our research group in Edmonton, has incorporated some of our group's work in this area in its Poker Academy software.

Although this program plays poker pretty well, it can't yet do what is most required—spot and exploit the other player's weaknesses. Figuring out how to program a computer to do that is extraordinarily hard. Why so? Studying an opponent should be easy, after all—and it is, but only if you have thousands of poker hands to analyze. What do you do if you have only a few? To make matters worse, human poker players make a point of changing their style so as to be hard to predict.

Right now, the best poker-playing programs to come out of our research group will make money off your average human player, and they are beginning to beat even some of the best in the world in organized competitions. This suggests that poker is just now joining the ranks of chess and checkers—games at which computers have trounced even world champions.

One lesson that computer scientists learned from working on chess and checkers is that programs must strike a balance in how they decide what move to make next. At one extreme, the computer can look all the way to the end of a game, examine every possible final position, and evaluate whether each one constitutes a win, a draw, or a loss. Then it can work backward from those possibilities, assuming best play by both sides at every stage, to select the optimal move. But searching that far ahead would take a great deal of time—for chess, enough for the sun to burn out.

The alternative is to use an evaluation function that incorporates knowledge of the game, enough to go beyond just recognizing an outright win to sense, rather, the slightest inkling of an advantage. In the ideal case, such a program would play perfectly while looking only a single move ahead. Of course, such a sophisticated evaluation would also require a lot of computational power.

In actuality, chess-playing programs operate somewhere between these two extremes. The computer typically examines all the possibilities several moves ahead and evaluates each, say, by tallying points, having assigned a different number of points to a pawn, a knight, a rook, and so forth. The computer then works backward to the current board position. The result is a ranking of all the available next moves, making it easy to pick the best one.

The trade-off between blind searching and employing specialized knowledge is a central topic in AI research. In video games, searching can be problematic because there are often vast sets of possible game states to consider and not much time and memory available to make the required calculations. One way to get around these hurdles is to work not on the actual game at hand but on a much-simplified version. Abstractions of this kind often make it practical to search far ahead through the many possible game states while assessing each of them according to some straightforward formula. If that can be done, a computer-operated character will appear as intelligent as a chess-playing program—although the bot's seemingly deft actions will, in fact, be guided by simple brute-force calculations.

Take, for example, the problem of moving around intelligently in a virtual world—such as finding the shortest path to take from one spot to another. That's easy enough to figure out if you can fly like a crow. But what if you're earthbound and there are obstacles to contend with along the way?

A general algorithm for determining the best route between two points on a map has been around since the late 1960s. The problem with this scheme—known as A*—is that the amount of time the solution takes to compute scales with the size of the territory, and the domains of video games are normally quite large. So there isn't time to calculate the optimal path in this way. In some games, the computer needs to move hundreds—or even thousands—of bots around their virtual stomping grounds without the action grinding to a crawl, which means that computation times must often be kept to just a few milliseconds per bot.

To address this issue, our research group has developed a series of pathfinding algorithms that simplify the problem. Rather than considering each of the vast number of possible positions each bot can take, these algorithms seek good paths by using coarser versions of the game map. Some of these algorithms can use a set amount of time for planning each move, no matter how vast the playing field, so they can be applied to game worlds of any size and complexity. They are also suitable for environments that change frequently, for instance when paths are blocked, bridges destroyed, doors closed, and so forth. BioWare will be using some of our group's pathfinding algorithms in its forthcoming *Dragon Age: Origins*.

This same general approach can help computers master real-time strategy games, such as the *Warcraft* series, introduced in 1994, which was developed by Blizzard Entertainment of Irvine, Calif. In this popular genre, players control armies of game characters that work together to gather resources and battle enemies on uncharted terrain. The fast pace and large numbers of bots make these games too complex for today's AI systems to handle, at least at a level that would challenge good human players.

Our research tries to address this problem by considering only the relatively small set of high-level strategies each player can follow, such as having your army of characters rush the

opponent or expand aggressively so as to take over more territory. The computer simulates what the outcome would be,
given the current state of play, if each side picked one of these
strategies and kept to it for the duration of the game. By taking into account whether its human opponent is using all or
just a few particular strategies, the computer can choose the
counterstrategy that is most likely to succeed. This approach
works better than the scripted maneuvers computers now employ in real-time strategy games when pitted against a human
player.

The need for better AI in commercial video games is
readily apparent—especially to the people playing them. And
their thirst for more computer-generated intelligence will only
continue to grow. Yet game makers rarely have the time or resources to conduct the research required to solve the many
thorny problems involved, which is why they have come to
recognize the value of engaging the scholarly community—a
community that is hard at work in such places as Georgia
Tech; Simon Fraser University, in Burnaby, B.C., Canada; the
University of Teesside, in the UK; and the Technical University
of Lisbon, to name but a few of the many research centers
around the world involved in this kind of work.

With the increased participation of academics in game-
related AI research, it will not be long before major improvements are apparent in the quality of the games entering the
market. But there is a more significant reason to applaud the
growing interest of AI researchers in the video-game industry—something Laird and van Lent pointed out to us and
other computer scientists nearly a decade ago. The work we
must do to make games feel more realistic will also take us a
long way toward our ultimate goal of developing general-
purpose machine intelligence. Now that sounds like a smart
move.

> *"Like so much else in our technology-rich and innovation-poor modern world, chess computing has fallen prey to incrementalism and the demands of the market."*

Artificial Intelligence and Chess Have Not Necessarily Benefited One Another

Garry Kasparov

Garry Kasparov is a chess grandmaster and world champion. In the following viewpoint, he argues that the success of computers in playing chess has done little to increase understanding of the human mind or artificial intelligence (AI). Instead, he says, chess programmers have simply relied on computational power, abandoning the effort to reproduce or gain insight into human intelligence. Kasparov concludes with the hope that AI poker programs may produce more valuable results.

As you read, consider the following questions:

1. What is Kasparov's answer as to how many moves ahead in a chess game he sees?

Garry Kasparov, "The Chess Master and the Computer," *New York Review of Books*, February 11, 2010. Reprinted with permission.

2. What does Kasparov say we have discarded innovation and creativity in exchange for?

3. What might humans be able to relearn from poker, according to Kasparov?

The moment I became the youngest world chess champion in history at the age of twenty-two in 1985, I began receiving endless questions about the secret of my success and the nature of my talent. Instead of asking about Sicilian Defenses, journalists wanted to know about my diet, my personal life, how many moves ahead I saw, and how many games I held in my memory.

Talent Explains Little

I soon realized that my answers were disappointing. I didn't eat anything special. I worked hard because my mother had taught me to. My memory was good, but hardly photographic. As for how many moves ahead a grandmaster sees, [Diego] Russkin-Gutman [author of a book on chess and AI] makes much of the answer attributed to the great Cuban world champion José Raúl Capablanca, among others: "Just one, the best one." This answer is as good or bad as any other, a pithy way of disposing with an attempt by an outsider to ask something insightful and failing to do so. It's the equivalent of asking Lance Armstrong how many times he shifts gears during the Tour de France.

The only real answer, "It depends on the position and how much time I have," is unsatisfying. In what may have been my best tournament game at the 1999 Hoogovens tournament in the Netherlands, I visualized the winning position a full fifteen moves ahead—an unusual feat. I sacrificed a great deal of material for an attack, burning my bridges; if my calculations were faulty I would be dead lost. Although my intuition was correct and my opponent . . . failed to find the best defense under pressure, subsequent analysis showed that despite my

Herculean effort I had missed a shorter route to victory. Capablanca's sarcasm aside, correctly evaluating a small handful of moves is far more important in human chess, and human decision-making in general, than the systematically deeper and deeper search for better moves—the number of moves "seen ahead"—that computers rely on.

There is little doubt that different people are blessed with different amounts of cognitive gifts such as long-term memory and the visuospatial skills chess players are said to employ. One of the reasons chess is an "unparalleled laboratory" and a "unique nexus" is that it demands high performance from so many of the brain's functions. Where so many of these investigations fail on a practical level is by not recognizing the importance of the process of learning and playing chess. The ability to work hard for days on end without losing focus is a talent. The ability to keep absorbing new information after many hours of study is a talent. Programming yourself by analyzing your decision-making outcomes and processes can improve results much the way that a smarter chess algorithm will play better than another running on the same computer. We might not be able to change our hardware, but we can definitely upgrade our software.

The End of Innovation

With the supremacy of the chess machines now apparent and the contest of "Man vs. Machine" a thing of the past, perhaps it is time to return to the goals that made computer chess so attractive to many of the finest minds of the twentieth century. Playing better chess was a problem they wanted to solve, yes, and it has been solved. But there were other goals as well: to develop a program that played chess by thinking like a human, perhaps even by learning the game as a human does. Surely this would be a far more fruitful avenue of investigation than creating, as we are doing, ever-faster algorithms to run on ever-faster hardware.

This is our last chess metaphor, then—a metaphor for how we have discarded innovation and creativity in exchange for a steady supply of marketable products. The dreams of creating an artificial intelligence that would engage in an ancient game symbolic of human thought have been abandoned. Instead, every year we have new chess programs, and new versions of old ones, that are all based on the same basic programming concepts for picking a move by searching through millions of possibilities that were developed in the 1960s and 1970s.

Like so much else in our technology-rich and innovation-poor modern world, chess computing has fallen prey to incrementalism and the demands of the market. Brute-force programs play the best chess, so why bother with anything else? Why waste time and money experimenting with new and innovative ideas when we already know what works? Such thinking should horrify anyone worthy of the name of scientist, but it seems, tragically, to be the norm. Our best minds have gone into financial engineering instead of real engineering, with catastrophic results for both sectors.

Not Chess, but Poker

Perhaps chess is the wrong game for the times. Poker is now everywhere, as amateurs dream of winning millions and being on television for playing a card game whose complexities can be detailed on a single piece of paper. But while chess is a 100 percent information game—both players are aware of all the data all the time—and therefore directly susceptible to computing power, poker has hidden cards and variable stakes, creating critical roles for chance, bluffing, and risk management.

These might seem to be aspects of poker based entirely on human psychology and therefore invulnerable to computer incursion. A machine can trivially calculate the odds of every hand, but what to make of an opponent with poor odds making a large bet? And yet the computers are advancing here as well. Jonathan Schaeffer, the inventor of the checkers-solving program, has moved on to poker and his digital players are performing better and better against strong humans—with obvious implications for online gambling sites.

Perhaps the current trend of many chess professionals taking up the more lucrative pastime of poker is not a wholly negative one. It may not be too late for humans to relearn how to take risks in order to innovate and thereby maintain the advanced lifestyles we enjoy. And if it takes a poker-playing supercomputer to remind us that we can't enjoy the rewards without taking the risks, so be it.

Periodical and Internet Sources Bibliography

The following articles have been selected to supplement the diverse views presented in this chapter.

Amara D. Angelica	"New Supercomputer on a Chip 'Sees' Well Enough to Drive a Car Someday," www.kurzweilAI.net, September 16, 2010.
Daniel Dennett	"Higher Games," *Technology Review*, September/October 2007.
h+ Magazine	"Wired for War or How We Learned to Stop Worrying and Let Dystopian SF Movies Inspire Our Military Bots," May 20, 2009.
Richard A. Lovett	"Artificial Intelligence to Boost Space-Probe Efficiency," *National Geographic*, May 30, 2006.
John Markoff	"Google Cars Drive Themselves in Traffic," *New York Times*, October 9, 2010.
McKnight's	"Advanced MRI, Artificial Intelligence Techniques Help Identify Those at Risk for Further Cognitive Decline," October 7, 2010.
J.R. Minkel	"Robotics Prof Sees Threat in Military Robots," *Scientific American*, February 28, 2008.
Phil Patton	"Far Out: Studios Imagine Smart Cars for a World Transformed by Robots," *New York Times*, November 11, 2007.
Ure Paul	"Brief History of Video Game AI," www.actiontrip.com, January 25, 2008.
Roland Piquepaille	"AI Behind Smart Car Wheels," *ZDNet*, June 18, 2007.
Tim Weiner	"New Model Army Soldier Rolls Closer to Battle," *New York Times*, February 16, 2005.

For Further Discussion

Chapter 1

1. Vernor Vinge argues that humans soon will be able to create creatures that "surpass humans in every intellectual and creative dimension." Would John Horgan agree with this statement? Use examples to illustrate why he would agree or disagree.

2. Harry Plantinga argues that God gives humans a unique soul and that this belief affects how Christian scientists approach their work. Does he base this on a logical argument, on faith, or on both? Does Russell C. Bjork believe that faith or logic denies the possibility of an artificial intelligence with a soul? Explain your answer using examples.

3. The *Economist* suggests that artificial intelligence based on insects is possible. Considering the viewpoint by Russell and Norvig, would you agree that the applications discussed in the *Economist* article are actually artificial intelligence? Why or why not?

Chapter 2

1. Mark Halpern argues that the Turing Test is not useful in part because humans perform very poorly in the tests. Melissa Lafsky and Yaakov Menken also point out ways in which non-intelligent computer programs can fool judges. Can you think of ways to organize a Turing Test that would minimize the problem of human error? Is there any way to set up a test to determine if a computer is intelligent?

2. Paul R. Cohen argues that artificial intelligence (AI) programmers need challenging problems to focus their ef-

forts. Based on Cohen's suggestion, give an example of an AI problem that you would like to see researchers try to solve. Try to keep in mind Cohen's criteria for a good problem.

Chapter 3

1. Are Eliezer Yudkowsky's worries about unethical super-robots realistic based on the articles by Nic Fleming and Noel Sharkey and Joanna J. Bryson? Is it worth trying to defend against unethical super-robots even if the likelihood of the creation of such robots is very small? Why or why not?

2. John P. Sullins III presents three requirements of robot moral agency. Based on these requirements, would the (fictional) Eth-o-tron robots discussed by Drew McDermott qualify as moral agents? How might McDermott criticize Sullins' requirements?

Chapter 4

1. Mark Herman and Art Fritzson argue that artificial intelligence in the military might mean the end of the drill sergeant. They call this outcome "frightening." Do you agree with their assessment? Are there any other outcomes Herman and Fritzson discuss that seem more dangerous?

2. Garry Kasparov argues that focusing on games has led AI researchers to abandon more important tasks. What are those tasks? Would Jonathan Schaeffer and his coauthors agree with Kasparov on the correct focus for AI research?

Organizations to Contact

The editors have compiled the following list of organizations concerned with the issues debated in this book. The descriptions are derived from materials provided by the organizations. All have publications or information available for interested readers. The list was compiled on the date of publication of the present volume; the information provided here may change. Be aware that many organizations take several weeks or longer to respond to inquiries, so allow as much time as possible.

Association for the Advancement of Artificial Intelligence (AAAI)
445 Burgess Dr., Suite 100, Menlo Park, CA   94025
(650) 328-3123 • fax: (650) 321-4457
website: www.aaai.org

The Association for the Advancement of Artificial Intelligence, formerly the American Association for Artificial Intelligence, is a nonprofit scientific society devoted to advancing the scientific understanding of the mechanisms underlying thought and intelligent behavior and their embodiment in machines. AAAI also aims to increase public understanding of artificial intelligence (AI) and to improve the teaching and training of people working in the AI field. The organization publishes *AI Magazine* and the *Journal of Artificial Intelligence Research.* Many technical papers are available on its website in addition to an AI topics section containing extensive information for secondary school teachers and students.

Cato Institute
1000 Massachusetts Ave. NW, Washington, DC   20001-5403
(202) 842-0200 • fax: (202) 842-3490
website: www.cato.org

The Cato Institute is a public policy research organization dedicated to the principles of individual liberty, limited government, free markets, and peace. It publishes numerous reports and periodicals, including the *Cato Journal* and *Cato Policy Report*. Its website contains a searchable database of articles, news, and commentary, including "Hayek's Evolutionary Epistemology, Artificial Intelligence, and the Question of Free Will," and "Future Imperfect: Technology and Freedom in an Imperfect World."

Computing Research Association (CRA)

1828 L St. NW, Suite 800, Washington, DC   20036-4632
(202) 234-2111 • fax: (202) 667-1066
e-mail: info@cra.org
website: www.cra.org

The Computing Research Association seeks to strengthen research and education in the computing fields, expand opportunities for women and minorities, and educate the public and policy makers on the importance of computing research. CRA's publications include the bimonthly newsletter *Computing Research News*. The website includes other resources, such as memos on best practices and white papers on computing education issues.

Ethics + Emerging Sciences Group at California Polytechnic State

e-mail: palin@calpoly.edu
website: http://ethics.calpoly.edu

The Ethics + Emerging Sciences Group at California Polytechnic State is a nonpartisan organization focused on the risks, ethics, and social impacts of emerging sciences and technologies. The group organizes talks, engages in research, and publishes papers. Publications, including reports on military robots and human enhancement, are downloadable from its website.

Lifeboat Foundation

1638 Esmeralda Ave., Minden, NV   89423
(775) 329-0180 • fax: (775) 329-0190

e-mail: education@lifeboat.com
website: www.lifeboat.com

The Lifeboat Foundation is a nonprofit nongovernmental organization dedicated to encouraging scientific advancements
while helping humanity survive existential risks and possible
misuse of increasingly powerful technologies, including genetic engineering, nanotechnology, and robotics/artificial intelligence (AI). The organization's website contains a number
of articles about AI, such as "The Age of Virtuous Machines,"
"AI and Sci-fi," and "Can a Machine Be Conscious?" It also
publishes a newsletter, *Lifeboat News*.

Massachusetts Institute of Technology Computer Science and Artificial Intelligence Laboratory (CSAIL)

The Stata Center, Building 32, 32 Vassar St.
Cambridge, MA   02139
(617) 253-5851 • fax: (617) 258-8682
e-mail: webmaster@csail.mit.edu
website: www.csail.mit.edu

The mission of CSAIL is to conduct research in both computation and artificial intelligence (AI), broadly construed. News
and technical papers related to AI, as well as news reports and
updates, are available on its website.

Singularity Institute for Artificial Intelligence (SIAI)

PO Box 472079, San Francisco, CA   94147
e-mail: institute@singinst.org
website: www.singinst.org

The Singularity Institute for Artificial Intelligence is a nonprofit research institute that aims to ensure the development
of friendly artificial intelligence (AI) for the benefit of all
mankind; prevent unsafe AI from causing harm; and encourage rational thought about our future as a species. SIAI hosts
the annual Singularity Summit. Its website contains research
publications, videos of presentations and interviews, and a
blog.

Society for the Study of Artificial Intelligence and Simulation of Behaviour (SSAISB)

SSAISB Executive Office Chichester C1-209
School of Science and Technology
University of Sussex Falmer, Brighton   BN1 9QH
  United Kingdom
+44 (0) 1273 678448
e-mail: admin11@aisb.org.uk
website: www.aisb.org.uk

The Society for the Study of Artificial Intelligence and Simulation of Behaviour is the largest artificial intelligence (AI) society in the United Kingdom. It invites membership from people with a serious interest in AI, cognitive science, and related areas. SSAISB publishes the *AISB Quarterly*, *AISB Weekly Bulletin*, and the proceedings of AISB conventions, all of which are available on its website.

Special Interest Group for Computers and Society (SIGCAS)

c/o Association for Computing Machinery (ACM)
2 Penn Plz., Suite 701, New York, NY   10121-0701
Phone: (212) 626-0500 • fax: (212) 944-1318
e-mail: acmhelp@acm.org
website: www.sigcas.org

The Special Interest Group for Computers and Society, which is part of the Association for Computing Machinery, is composed of computer and physical scientists, professionals, and other individuals interested in addressing the social and ethical consequences of computer usage and informing the public about the impact of technology on society. It publishes the quarterly newsletter *Computers and Society*, which is available through its website.

University of Alberta GAMES Group

e-mail: jonathan@cs.ualberta.ca
website: http://webdocs.cs.ualberta.ca/~games/

The University of Alberta GAMES Group produces high-performance, real-time programs for strategic game playing. The group has developed programs in chess, checkers, poker, and other games. Its website contains discussions and information about its games in development, as well as links to group members' pages with publications.

Bibliography of Books

Ron Arkin

Governing Lethal Behavior in Autonomous Robots. Boca Raton, FL: Taylor & Francis Group, 2009.

Yoseph Bar-Cohen and David Hanson

The Coming Robot Revolution: Expectations and Fears About Emerging Intelligent, Humanlike Machines. New York: Springer Science and Business Media, 2009.

Henry Brighton

Introducing Artificial Intelligence. Cambridge, UK: Totem Books, 2003.

Matt Carter

Minds and Computers: An Introduction to the Philosophy of Artificial Intelligence. Edinburgh, UK: Edinburgh University Press, 2007.

Stacey L. Edgar

Morality and Machines: Perspectives on Computer Ethics. 2nd ed. Sudbury, MA: Jones & Bartlett Learning, 2002.

Robert Epstein, ed.

Parsing the Turing Test: Philosophical and Methodological Issues in the Quest for the Thinking Computer. New York: Springer Science and Business Media, 2009.

Anne Foerst

God in the Machine: What Robots Teach Us About Humanity and God. New York: Oxford University Press, 2004.

Sandy Fritz, ed.

Understanding Artificial Intelligence. New York: Warner Books, 2002.

Robert Geraci

Apocalyptic AI: Visions of Heaven in Robotics, Artificial Intelligence, and Virtual Reality. New York: Oxford University Press, 2010.

J. Storrs Hall

Beyond AI: Creating the Conscience of the Machine. Amherst, NY: Prometheus Books, 2007.

David Harel

Computers Ltd: What They Really Can't Do. New York: Oxford University Press, 2000.

Jeff Hawkins

On Intelligence. New York: Henry Holt and Company, 2005.

John Horgan

The Undiscovered Mind: How the Human Brain Defies Replication, Medication, and Explanation. New York: Touchstone, 1999.

Feng-hsiung Hsu

Behind Deep Blue: Building the Computer That Defeated the World Chess Champion. Princeton, NJ: Princeton University Press, 2002.

James Kennedy, Russell C. Eberhart, and Yuhui Shi

Swarm Intelligence. San Francisco: Morgan Kaufmann Publications, 2001.

Ray Kurzweil

The Singularity Is Near: When Humans Transcend Biology. New York: Penguin Group, 2005.

Marvin Minsky

The Emotion Machine: Commonsense Thinking, Artificial Intelligence, and the Future of the Human Mind. New York: Simon & Schuster, 2007.

Marvin Minsky   *The Society of Mind.* New York:
                  Simon & Schuster, 1988.

Charles Petzold   *The Annotated Turing: A Guided Tour
                  Through Alan Turing's Historic Paper
                  on Computability and the Turing
                  Machine.* Indianapolis, IN: Wiley
                  Publishing, 2008.

Diego   *Chess Metaphors: Artificial Intelligence
Rasskin-Gutman   and the Human Mind,* translated by
                  Deborah Klosky. Cambridge, MA:
                  MIT Press, 2009.

Jonathan   *Chips Challenging Champions: Games,
Schaeffer   Computers, and Artificial Intelligence.*
and Jaap   Amsterdam, Holland: North Holland
van den Herik   Press, 2002.

Stuart Shieber   *The Turing Test: Verbal Behavior as
                  the Hallmark of Intelligence.*
                  Cambridge, MA: MIT Press, 2004.

P.W. Singer   *Wired for War: The Robotics
                  Revolution and Conflict in the 21st
                  Century.* New York: Penguin Press,
                  2009.

Wendell Wallach   *Moral Machines: Teaching Robots
                  Right from Wrong.* New York: Oxford
                  University Press, 2008.

Blay Whitby   *Artificial Intelligence: A Beginner's
                  Guide.* Oxford, UK: Oneworld
                  Publications, 2008.

Index